The
Books of the Beast

Essays on
Aleister Crowley, Montague Summers
and others

Timothy d'Arch Smith

Mandrake

The
Books of the Beast

Essays on
Aleister Crowley, Montague Summers
and others

Timothy d'Arch Smith

Mandrake

The
Books of the Beast

Timothy d'Arch Smith is a well-known bibliographer, reviewer and antiquarian bookseller with a special interest in the by-ways of literature, notably the occult and the curious. His other interests include cricket and American popular music.

British Library Cataloguing in Publication Data
d'Arch Smith, Timothy 1936-
Books of the Beast: Essays on Aleister Crowley, Montague Summers, Ralph Chubb and others. 2nd.ed.
1. English literature. Special subjects. Occultism
I. Title
820.937
ISBN 1-86992-817-2

Contents

Sometimes I think
Life is just a rodeo
The trick is to ride
And make it to the bell

John Fogerty

Preface

The article on the Fortune Press introduced the handlist of the Press's publications published by Bertram Rota (London 1983); 'Ralph Nicholas Chubb' was printed as an appendix to my *Love in Earnest* (Routledge & Kegan Paul, 1970). 'Florence Farr' was written as a Foreword to the reprint of her *Egyptian Magic* issued by the Aquarian Press (Wellingborough, 1982). Montague Summers was printed in a limited edition by the Tragara Press (Edinburgh, 1984). 'The Wood from Detritus' appeared under a different title in *The Times Literary Supplement* (29 May 1981).

It is a pleasure to acknowledge the help and encouragement of Miss Jean Overton Fuller; Miss Clare Layton; Mr Robert Booth; Mr R A Gilbert; Mr Francis King; Mr Peter Mendes; Mr Jimmy Page; Mr Anthony Powell CH; Mr Robert Rees; Mr G F Sims; the staff of the Warburg Institute, London; of the Manuscripts Department of University College London; and of the British Library.

For this revised edition, the title essay has benefited enormously from help given and howlers corrected by Mr Martin Starr. I have removed an essay on Francis Barrett and replaced it with another one on Crowley: '"Dr Trelawney" and Aleister Crowley' first appeared in *London Magazine*, March 1988.

1

'The Books of the Beast'

Prolegomena to a Bibliography of Aleister Crowley

1

'MAGICK', wrote Aleister Crowley in *Magick in Theory and Practice*, 'is the Science and Art of causing Change to occur in conformity with Will.' If we accept, and we must if we are to begin to understand the nature of the man, his belief in the efficacy of magic–with or without the 'k'–it will come as no surprise that not infrequently he brought magical techniques to bear on the success of his literary work. Rather it should surprise us if we found no evidence of that kind, no ceremonies performed, no prayers offered, no spirits evoked, in the pursuit of literary inspiration and fluency; if, from the printed books that supplied the general public with that inspiration and that fluency, he expected no magical bestowal of wealth and fame. When, therefore, we discover in his diaries for 1914-20[1] notes on rituals performed for good fortune to his Simon Iff stories[2], for 'literary current', for 'success in Shaw article[3]', for 'poetic inspiration', we must accept it as no odder than discovering in another man's diaries that he has gone to church and prayed to God to bless his endeavours. When we learn from the 1923 diary[4] that he was wont to consult the Chinese oracle, the *I Ching*, for guidance concerning similar matters, this, too, we have to take for granted. Stephen Skinner, editor of that diary, has counted in the preceding (1914-1920) records, as many as eighteen operations that can be bracketed under the heading of 'literary success.'

The bibliographer of Crowley, however, might be forgiven if he felt that sort of acceptance outside his brief, although, as he goes about his business, he will find himself obliged to apply biographical information of a less arcane kind to the task in hand. Few authors have had the chance–in early days, the money–so precisely to dictate how they wanted their books produced. That, he will need to inform us, is why they are so striking. Only when Crowley had no say in their manufacture do they become either workaday, like *Diary of a Drug Fiend* (1922), or–like *Songs for Italy* (1923)–

9

just plain ghastly. In most cases Crowley's hand can be seen at work in every stage of the book's production; and a perceptive bibliographer will pinpoint from biographical sources how and why and through whose influence Crowley came to choose the materials he did. Yet to do his subject justice, he must, however distastefully, when applying his science, keep in his sights that premise of Crowley's that magic actually works. I am not referring to the sigils and seals that adorn covers and title-pages and imprimaturs, the heptagonal seal of the A∴A∴, the dove and chalice device of the O∴T∴O∴, the foreshortened phallus, the rayed eye in the triangle, which endow a certain mystical quality, but to an intrinsic symbolism Crowley built in to the very heart of his publications. For the books themselves, the books as artifacts, that is–as physical objects, their paper, their size, their colour, their price (we can go so far)–reflect as much as their contents their author's magical philoso-phies; and those a bibliographer of Aleister Crowley must interpret and clarify for him who will consult his work.

For this reason–that bibliographical duties, as well as offering factual data, must also propound non-technical, indeed irrational, concepts–this essay is divided into two parts, occult and mundane. We can do no better, in opening the occult section, than to continue the quotation of Crowley's theory of magic. He at once gives us the clue that has been hinted at above:

> Illustration: It is my Will to inform the World of certain facts within my knowledge. I therefore take 'magical weapons', pen, ink and paper; I write 'incantations'–these sentences–in the 'magical language' i.e. that which is understood by the people I wish to instruct; I call forth 'spirits', such as printers, publishers, booksellers, and so forth, and constrain them to convey my message to those people. The composition and distribution of this book is thus an act of MAGICK by which I cause Changes to take place in conformity with my Will.[5]

Magick appeared in 1930.[6] By then Crowley had travelled a long road. He was fifty-five years old. He had founded his own magical order, the A∴A∴, in 1907 and had become the English head of another, the O∴T∴O∴, in 1912. Yet rail against it though he might (and did), it was the magical order he had joined as a young man of twenty-three, the Order of the Golden Dawn, that exerted, throughout his life, the very strongest influence; and it is in the light of that Order's teaching that we must study Crowley's attitude towards the printed book, its make-up, its design, and the way he launched it upon the world.

Certain documents, known as the 'Z' documents, were circulated among Golden Dawn members to elucidate the symbolism of the ritual of initiation or Neophyte grade. In Z2 we find a most illuminating sentence: 'For this Ritual betokeneth a certain Person, Substance or *Thing* [my italics], which is taken from the dark World of Matter, to be brought under the operation of the Divine Formulae of the Magic of Light.'[7] Herein lies the first clue that objects as well as human beings can be initiated and subjected to change. Now the closest object to a book discoverable in Golden Dawn rituals is a talisman. This is described in the formal Order instructions as 'a magical figure charged with the force which it is intended to represent. In the construction of a Talisman, care should be taken to make it, as far as possible, so to represent the Universal Forces that it should be in exact harmony with those you wish to attract, and the more exact the symbolism, the more easy it is to attract the force–other things coinciding, such as consecration at the right time, etc.'[8] Instructions are elsewhere given[9] for a talisman consecrated to Jupiter and it is here that we find repeated, almost word for word, spoken over the object, the sentences spoken to the Candidate in the Neophyte ritual:

> Take the Talisman, and circumambulate. After going round once, stop in the South, and place it on ground.

> 'Unpurified and unconsecrated, thou canst not enter the gate of the West.' Purify the Talisman with Water and consecrate with Fire.

Referring to the Neophyte ritual[10] we find the following instructions on the initiation of a human being. In freemasonic style, the candidate, blind-folded and in the presence of eleven officers of the Order, is undergoing ritual ordeals and being aurally supplied with items of occult information.

> Hierophant.[11] 'Let the Mystical Circumambulation take place in the Path of Knowledge that leadeth into Light, with the Lamp of Hidden Knowledge to guide us.'

> Kerux.[12] Stops in the South after the second passing of the Hierophant and barring the way with his Wand, says: 'Unpurified and Unconsecrated, though canst not enter the path of the West.'

The candidate is now on the brink of initiation. A third officer, Hegemon,[13] declaims:

> 'Inheritor of a Dying World, we call thee to the Living Beauty.'

> Hiereus.[14] 'Wanderer in the Wild Darkness, we call thee to the Gentle Light.' (The blindfold is removed).

> Hiero. 'Long hast thou dwelt in Darkness–Quit the Night and seek the Day.'

Returning again to the talisman-consecrating ritual we find that at its climax the magician, echoing the Hierophant's bidding to the Neophyte and unwrapping the talisman from a silken covering in the same way as the candidate's blindfolded eyes are uncovered at this point, cries out to the talisman: 'Creature of Talismans, long hast thou dwelt in darkness. Quit the night and seek the day.'[15]

The similarities are clear. The talisman, no less than the initiate, is a 'creature' about to go up a scale on the evolutionary ladder. Indeed, all magical implements in the Golden Dawn–the cup, the wand, the dagger, the pentacle, the sword, the Rose-Cross lamen, and the lotus-wand–were 'subjected' to the Neophyte ritual to imbue them with the necessary magical current. It is in this way, in his conception of a book as a talisman, that we must follow Crowley's ideas about book publishing. The book, like the talisman, was born into the world to propagate the Great Work. Although by no means all his books have 'talismanic' virtues, by further reference to Golden Dawn instructions we can discover which of them do.

The manufacture of a talisman demanded astrological calculations, hours when certain planets were exalted or when the sun was in certain zodiacal signs that would favour the purpose for which it was being prepared. In many cases Crowley has given us–on the title-pages, so there can be no doubt of his intentions–this exact time. Apart from one (the first separate) edition of *The Book of the Law* (Tunis, 1926), which is dated Sol in 18°32'45" Aries, Luna in 7°16'55" Pisces,[16] perhaps because Crowley felt Sun sextile Jupiter especially propitious, he preferred to publish at the exact moment of the spring or autumn equinox or at the summer or winter solstice. There are excellent magical reasons for choosing these moments, ones he also learned in the Golden Dawn. The ceremony of the Equinox[17] was for the nomination of new officers and was a biannual re-affirmation of the aims of the Order, Crowley's 'talismanic' publications re-affirming in like manner his own aims and aspirations. Indeed, his biannual magazine was called *The Equinox* and the Sun-sigil and the sigils for the equinoctial signs of Aries and Libra appear on title-pages and spines. Times are sometimes more precisely given. *England, Stand Fast!*, Crowley's patriotic poem composed on the outbreak of war, is dated 'September 23, 1939, e.v. [Era Vulgaris, the Christian Era as opposed to the 'Thelemic' one which commenced with the reception of *The Book of the Law*, designated 'Anno 0', in 1904], 10.50 p.m.,' the very second the sun moved from Virgo into Libra. *The Book of Thoth* bears the date 'An Ixviii[18] Sol in 0°0'0" Aries March 21, 1944 e.v. 5.29 p.m.' For *Olla*, his second anthology of poetry (the first, *Ambergris*, not a talismanic publication, came out in 1910), he chose a solsticial publication date, the shortest day in layman's terms, 'Sol in 0° Capricornus Dec. 22, 10.54 a.m.' *Temperance* (6.6 p.m. 22 December 1939), *The Fun of the Fair* (11.31 a.m. 22 December 1942), and *The City of God* (12.3 p.m. 21 March 1943) are other examples of astrological publication dates.

Of all the various symbolisms employed by the Golden Dawn, by far the most important was the one of colour. The moment the blindfold was removed from the candidate's eyes in the Neophyte ceremony, the presence of colours, many and varied, in the robes, the magical implements, the Temple altar and its walls, impressed itself in the most forceful way. On the lowest level, the symbolism is obvious: red for fire, black for earth, blue for water, yellow for air, white for Spirit: but a document circulated to candidates of the sixth, Adeptus Minor, Grade, 'The Book of the Path of the Chameleon,'[19] enormously elaborated on this and stressed the importance of correct colour symbolism for practical and meditative purposes. As every artist knows, each colour has its complementary, red-green, blue-orange, yellow-purple, a fact that the Golden Dawn raised from an optical truism to a magical phenomenon; and the illusion induced by staring at (say, a red square and then, by switching focus to a white surface, perceiving its complementary, green, took on great occult significance. These complementaries were known as 'flashing' colours, which, 'if joined to the original, enables it to attract, to a certain extent, the Akasic ['astral', a Theosophical term] current from the atmosphere, and to a certain extent from yourself, thus forming a vortex that can attract its flashing light from the atmosphere.'[20] What all this actually meant in practical terms was that all painted objects should 'flash', so the red fire wand was inscribed with green lettering, the blue water cup with orange, the yellow air dagger with purple; and talismans too were to be drawn in correct complementary colours. It is this teaching Crowley had in mind when he produced certain books bound in coloured cloths with complementary letterings. Thus we find *The Heart of the Master* (1938) bound in yellow cloth blocked in purple; *The Equinox,* III, 1 (Detroit 1919) bound in blue blocked in orange; and some copies of the 1936 edition of *The Book of the Law* bound with a blue spine and orange paper boards. There are other, not so obvious examples. *Konx om Pax* (1907) sub-titled 'Essays in Light', is bound in black cloth with white blocking, an affirmation of light out of darkness.[21] The two volumes of *Orpheus: a Lyrical Legend* (1905) are more complicated. There are five 'editions', actually all from one typesetting and so designated to impart to the purchaser a false idea of the book's popularity. (This was quite a common technique to promote sales, the most notorious being Fergus Hume's *Mystery of a Hansom Cab* (1888), the first–probably the sole–printing of which bears statements such as 'One Hundred and Seventy-Fifth Thousand' and other massive and misleading print numbers.) Crowley was to do the same thing with *The Sword of Song* ('Benares', actually Paris, 1904) dividing up a print run of only a hundred copies into four 'editions'[22], and *Why Jesus Wept* ('London', i.e. Paris, 1904) into five. The five 'editions' of *Orpheus* are bound in the five elemental colours: the first in white boards (for spirit), the second in yellow (for air), the fourth in blue (for water), the fifth in olive-green (for earth). I have never seen a copy of the 'third' edition, but we may assume it was bound in red for fire. There seems to be a discrepancy here since, as already stated, black was the earth elemental colour; but in fact the Golden Dawn taught that in the 'Queen' scale of colours (one of four scales) it was sub-divided into four, red mixed with black ('fire of earth'), which gives russet; yellow with black ('air of earth'), giving citrine; black with black ('earth of earth'), and blue with black ('water of earth'), giving olive-green. The symbolism is therefore correct.

It is a magical tradition that talismans, if not of wood or metal, should be inscribed on vellum: 'virgin parchment' is a common phrase in the old 'grimoires' or grammars of magic. It is, thus, not surprising, bibliophilic considerations apart, that Crowley issued a certain number of his more exalted texts on that material.[23] *The Holy Books* are an example. They are certain hieratic texts written by Crowley in his persona of V.V.V.V.V., a Master of the Temple of his own order, the A∴A∴. Bibliographically confusing, they are six in number, and all exist printed on vellum.

Volume 1: Liber LXI vel Causae and Liber Cordis Cincti Serpente.

Volume 2: Liber Liberi vel Lapis Lazuli.

Volume 3: Liber L vel Legis, Liber DCCCXIII[24] vel Ararita and Liber Trigrammaton.

They are handsome duodecimos, each page printed within a heavy gold border, and are bound in gold-blocked vellum. With both internal and external use of gold, Crowley is making an important magical point. Gold is the colour of the sixth 'emanation' on the Tree of Life, *Tiphareth* (Beauty), one of its many correspondences being 'Devotion to the Great Work'. White is the colour of the first 'emanation', *Kether* (the Crown), wherein consummation of the Great Work is achieved.[25]

Quite properly, a single copy of Crowley's and S.L MacGregor Mathers' edition of *The Book of the Goetia of Solomon the King* (Boleskine,[26] 1904) was printed on vellum. It is spectacular. Its vellum cover, inscribed 'Perdurabo 6=5 R.R. et A.C.[27] hoc opus dignefecit,' is decorated with a red pen-and-ink drawing of Crowley invoking the demon Paimon, and in the margins of the text are drawings of seven of the other spirits mentioned in the grimoire: Belial, Agares, Samigina (or Gamigin), Amon, Foras, Furfur, and Vepar.

Even the size of Crowley's books can have magical significance. *Book Four* is a case in point, although ideas were not completely carried through. Crowley writes in his *Confessions*: 'The number 4 being the formula of the book, it was of course to consist of four parts. I carried out this idea by expressing the number of the Tetrad, not only by the name and plan of the book, but by issuing it in the shape of a square 4 inches by 4, and pricing each part as a function of 4.'[28] To begin with this worked. *Book Four*, Parts I and

II by Frater Perdurabo (Crowley) and Soror Virakam (Mary d'Este Sturges)(London, Wieland), although not four inches by four inches, are in a square format. *Part I* was priced at four groats or one shilling, *Part II* at four tanners or two shillings. Like the *Holy Books* they, curiously, are not dated, but Crowley's disciple J. F. C. Fuller wrote an acquisition date in his copy of *Part One* of 8 December 1912.[29] *Part Two* appeared the following year. Then the scheme began to go wrong. *Part Three* was indeed issued in four fascicules, *'Magick in Theory and Practice by the Master Therion'*, but the leaf-measurements were 11 1/8 and 7 5/8 inches and instead of costing '4 "Lloyd George groats" (at this time the demagogue was offering the workman ninepence for fourpence, by means of an insurance swindle intended to enslave him more completely than ever)'[30] was priced at two guineas.

Despite the importance of *Magick* to Crowley–one of his longest books and nearly sixteen years in the making–practical problems overset 'talismanic' considerations he had hoped would ensure the book's success. He wrote to an unnamed correspondent, perhaps C. K. Ogden of *Basic English* fame, from Paris on 5 November 1928: 'The latest date of publication is the day of the Spring Equinox next year, and in view of certain facts of a magical character, with which I need not bother you.'[31] Even before that he had designed a special talisman to be reproduced on the covers [32] but his disciple Fra. N∴, who had been entrusted with the book's production, was having trouble finding a printer. Owing to a smear campaign against Crowley in the English press, his name if not mud was not far off it and word had reached a Scottish printing firm he had hoped would do the work that there would be trouble about it: 'The All-High Commissar of the Soviet in Edingrad disapproves of the manuscript after a month's masterly inactivity,' wrote Crowley to Fra. N∴ on 22 October 1928. This was presumably Turnbull & Spears, who had printed books for Crowley's 'Society for the Propagation of Religious Truth' based in Inverness-shire, *The Star and the Garter* (1904) and *Orpheus: a Lyrical Legend* (1905) among them, and to whom it seemed that Crowley had once owed, perhaps still did owe, part of a printing bill.[33] Towards the end of 1928 Crowley decided to have the book printed in Paris, where he was then living and approached Marcel Estiez who directed the Lecram Press at 26 rue d'Hautpont. He accepted Estiez's estimate of thirty francs a copy for 2,950 copies. Fra N∴, who had agreed to put up eight hundred pounds and to guarantee another thousand to get *Magick* printed, remitted three hundred on account and printing got under way. A print-run of 3,000 was decided upon.[34] Crowley chose the paper for the wrappers on 4 February 1929 and the first pages of proofs were delivered on 14 or 15 February 1929. Prospectuses were despatched to Parisian booksellers handling English titles–Smith's, Brentano's, Galignani, Sylvia Beach's Shakespeare & Co., and William Titus who had issued Crowley's translation of Baudelaire,[35] but not until well after the date of the equinox, on 12 April 1929, did Crowley have an advance copy in his hands. It is not clear why Fra. N∴ did not then settle Lecram's account–perhaps because the advanced three hundred had not been handed over but spent on brandy and cigars–but as late as 10 December 1929 the 3,000 copies of *Magick* were still unbound. On this date a document was drawn up, 'Proposal for the Establishment of a Financial Syndicate to Organize Production and Sale of Books by Aleister Crowley,'[36] and the stock was transferred to the Mandrake Press in London and only in 1930 put on the market.

Part Four of *Book Four* was to have been *The Book of the Law* and although printing had commenced as early as 1927 it proved abortive. Nevertheless, an edition of this book was given priority and we must now look at its various publications in the same 'magical' light we have applied up to now.

Holiest of the Holy Books, oracularly delivered by a being calling himself Aiwaz or Aiwass (both spellings are significant) in Cairo between the hours of noon and one p.m. on 8, 9 and 10 April 1904, it confirms Crowley as the prophet of a new aeon. Its hieratic message and qabalistic complexities were to concern Crowley for the rest of his life and they formed the basis for his magical order, the A∴A∴. It is best before going on to summarize the various editions:

BL1   London, 1909.

BL2   London, March 1912, in Crowley's magazine *The Equinox*, I, 7,
p.386.

BL3   London, September 1913, in *The Equinox*, I, 10, pp.9-33.

BL4   Tunis, 1926.

BL5   London, 1927.

BL6   London, 1936.

BL7   London, 1937.

BL8   London, 1938.

BL9   Pasadena, [31 October 1942].

BL1 is, as we have seen, part of Volume Three of *The Holy Books*.

BL2 consists only of a folding plate reproducing the original manuscript (much reduced) facing p.386 of the magazine. There is no letterpress transcription of the text and the handwriting is barely legible. Nonetheless, Crowley considered this to have been a 'ritualistic' publication as falling 'nine months' (presumably a gestation period) 'before the outbreak of the Balkan War, which broke up the West'.[37]

BL3. This publication Crowley considered even more earth-shaking than BL2: 'The second blow was struck by the re-publication of the Book in September 1913, and this time the might of this Magick burst out and caused a catastrophe to civilization.'[38] It was, of course, nine months before the outbreak of the First World War. By now Crowley had become convinced of the authority of Aiwaz's utterance and accepted its every precept as dogma. He read with attention four of Aiwaz's injunctions: 'My scribe Anhk-af-na-khonsu, the priest of the princes [i.e. Crowley] shall not in one letter change this book' (Chapter I, stanza 36). Eighteen verses on Aiwaz repeats the warning: 'Change not as much as the style of a letter; for behold! thou, o prophet, shalt not behold all these mysteries hidden therein.' Later Aiwaz becomes even more specific:

> All this and a book to say how thou didst come hither and a reproduction of this ink and paper for ever–for in it is the word secret & not only in the English–and thy comment upon this the Book of the Law shall be printed beautifully in red ink and black upon beautiful paper made by hand; and to each man and woman that thou meetest, were it but to dine or to drink at them, it is the Law to give. [Chapter III, stanza 39.]

Finally Aiwaz bids: 'This book shall be translated into all tongues; but always with the original in the writing of the Beast; for in the chance shape of the letters and their position to one another: in these are mysteries that no Beast shall divine.'(III, 47.)

Typographically, therefore, there was only one choice open to Crowley: to issue the original manuscript in a decent facsimile. 'When', he wrote in 1922 (published in *Magick*, 1930), '*The Book of the Law* and its comment is published with the forces of His whole Will in perfect obedience to the instructions which have up to now been misunderstood or neglected [i.e, no facsimile in BL1 and BL3 and an unreadably miniscule one in BL2] the result will be incalculably effective. The event will establish the kingdom of the Crowned and Conquering Child over the whole earth, and all men shall bow to the Law, which is "Love under Will".' BL4 was a step in the right direction. The sixty-five leaves of manuscript, paginated 1-22, [1] 2-22, 1-21, were photographed and printed, reduced (contrary, still, to Aiwaz's requirements) on photographic paper, and housed in a scarlet leather-covered box with a fitted lid. The title-leaf, correctly on handmade paper and printed in red and black, reads: 'A.L. Liber Legis. The Book of the Law sub figura XXXI[39] as delivered...to Ankh-af-na-khonsu the Priest of the Princes who is

666. Now privately issued after 22 years of preparation to eleven persons. Anno 02^{40} Sol in 18°32'41'45" Aries Luna in 7°16'55" Pisces [i.e. 9 April]. From the Lair of the Lion.' The limitation page is most revealing for it prints a list of eight of the eleven people to whom copies were presented:

'No.1. To 777-418' [Charles Stansfeld Jones, 'Fra. Achad', an important American disciple].

'No.2. To 156: 31-666-31; 667' [Leah Hirsig, 'Alostrael', one of Crowley's mistresses met in America in 1918 and for a time a 'Scarlet Woman' or priestess].

'No.3. To Saturnus' [Karl Germer, a German disciple, financial supporter and publisher of German translations of Crowley's works].

'No.4. To 516' [Jane Wolfe, a film actress, 'Soror Estai'].

'No.5. To Ich Will: O.G.' [Otto Gebhardi, so identified, as are the other recipients, by Fra. N.·., in his copy, No.11, Warburg Institute].

'No.6. To 666' [Crowley].

'No.7. To 666-14' [Dorothy Olsen, the Scarlet Woman who replaced Leah Hirsig]. In Chicago in 1931, an American disciple, Cecil Frederick Russell (Fra. Genesthai) issued photographic reproductions from this copy. Bibliographically speaking, they would constitute a second impression of BL4.

'No. 8. To ΘΣα [Dorothea Walker].

Then follow the copies for sale and their prices: No. 9 at £93; No. 10 at 418 US dollars; No. 11 at its equivalent in German Reichsmarks, Rm2542, the copy presented to or more likely paid for by Fra. N.·. £93 and $418 are far more than arbitrary or simply extortionate figures. Like the pricing of the 'Blue' Equinox (Detroit, 1919) at 666 cents and the quarto-divisible sums charged for *Book Four, Parts One* and *Two*, they have deeply significant meanings. To begin with, Crowley believed the Law's messenger was spelled Aivas, its Hebrew numerical equivalent being 78, the number too of *Mezla*, the influence from the highest Sephira on the Tree of Life, *Kether*, and of course the number of cards in the Tarot pack. Just before BL4, it was revealed to him that the correct spelling was Aiwaz, which in Hebrew yields 93. '418' is the numerical equivalent of yet another, Greek, spelling of Aiwaz, 'AIFASS'. The Reichsmarks price is also symbolic. 2542 is the Greek qabalistic number of the Delphic Oracle of the Law: see *Liber MCCLXIV* by Aleister Crowley et al. (London, Albion Lodge O.T.O., 1989).

Such a tiny number of copies could not go very far to promulgate the Law of Thelema, nor, since the manuscript had had to be photographically reduced, did it even yet conform to Aiwaz's specifications; so Crowley began to make arrangements for a more satisfactory edition, larger in both number and in format: BL5. Each facsimile leaf of manuscript was to be captioned by a letterpress transcription of the words upon it, but the scheme fell through and only the proofs, sixty-six leaves, survive in Fra. N∴'s collection at the Warburg Institute.

(About the same time another 'magical' book was being posited, a manual of geomancy, a method of divination by the use of earth much favoured by the Golden Dawn.[42] Had it appeared it would have become one of the most bizarre of *livres-objets,* for it was to be accompanied by a box painted in 'flashing' colours filled with sand–'We'll import a load from Mecca or Jerusalem,' Crowley wrote to Fra. N∴,[43]–in which with a pointed stick, also coloured, the enquirer stuck random holes that would yield a pattern of points from which an answer to his enquiry could be found. This, too, came to nothing.)

However, in 1936, its issue date again ritualistic since it precipitated, according to Crowley, after the statutory nine-month gestation period, 'the outbreak of the Sino-Japanese War,'[44] BL6 came out at the autumn equinox as Vol. III, No. 3 of Crowley's periodical *The Equinox.* For some time the magazine had included as supplements separate books by Crowley and had been threatening to become top-heavy. Vol. I, No 7 (March 1912), for instance, was too bulky for one printing firm on its own to manage in the given time and typesetting had been shared by Crowley's favourite firm, the Chiswick Press and the firm he later approached to print *Magick,* Turnbull & Spears of Edinburgh.[45] Furthermore, its appearance had been erratic, in fact had ceased altogether. Vol. I had been issued regularly enough at the equinoxes of the years 1909-1913 (ten numbers in all), but Vol. II had never seen the light of day. (Crowley neatly covered up the lacuna by calling it 'a volume of silence'.) Vol. III, No. 1, known as the 'Blue' Equinox because of the colour of its cloth cover and constituting, as we have seen a 'flashing' binding, was published in Detroit (Crowley was in the States from 1914-9) in March 1919, but most copies had been lost when the publishers, the Universal Publishing Company, went bankrupt. Reviving *The Equinox* with such an important text was an excellent idea.[46] Crown quarto in size, printed in 16pt Bembo on Crowley's favourite (Japanese) paper, handsomely bound in white buckram, gold-blocked by Spalding & Hodge, successors to the firm who had executed many fine art-nouveau bindings for John Lane and other firms in the 1890s, BL6 was a sumptuous production. The Comment, theretofore only a page or so, was expanded to a hundred-page essay, 'Genesis Libri Al'. The facsimile manuscript, printed full-size for the first time, was inserted into a pocket let into the book's back cover. It retailed at a guinea. There was a cheaper edition of 250 copies on machine-made paper cased in a plain, although 'flashing', binding of blue-cloth-backed orange paper boards at eleven shillings. 'This edition will be more valuable than the £1.1.0 one,' wrote Crowley to Fra. N∴.[47] The 'ritual' imprint on the title read: 'An Ix Sol in Libra September MCMXXXVI E.V. Issued by the O.T.O., BM/JPKH London, W.C.1'. There is an errata slip (of course) correcting, among other misprints, an unfortunate slip where the coloured frontispiece of the Stélé of Revealing was miscaptioned 'Stélé of Revelling'.

Production costs had been nearly four hundred pounds[48] but the book sold steadily and a reprint was put in hand the following year.[49] BL7 is superficially identical with the white buckram issue of 1936 but can be identified by a slip pasted over the imprint changing the date and the O.T.O. box-number. This reads 'An I xi Sol in Capricorn December MCMXXXVII E.V. Privately issued by the O.T.O. BCM/ANKH 188 High Holborn, W.C.2.' Further misprints had been spotted and a new errata slip of seventeen items replaces the original one of ten. The solsticial publication date is again ritualistic, nine months before what Crowley called the 'Betrayal' and we know as Munich, 30 September 1938. Furthermore, in order to comply with Aiwaz's command that the Book was for all mankind, a bizarre publication party was arranged. On the eve of 21 December, Crowley rounded up representatives of the white, black, brown, red, and yellow races–according to William Hickey's column in the *Daily Express* the next day the black representative was a dancing-girl, the Indian a non-English-speaking Bengali Muslim 'who seemed rather puzzled by the whole business'–and at the foot of Cleopatra's needle at precisely 6.22 a.m. on 22 December as the sun moved into Capricorn, presented each with a copy of BL7. Acceptance was briefly delayed while Crowley made a short speech:

Do what thou wilt shall be the whole of the law. I Ankh-f-n-khonsu, the Priest of the Princes, present you,——, as representative of your race, with the Book of the Law. It is the charter of Universal Freedom, for every man and woman in the world. Love is the law. Love under will.

Fra. N∴, also present together with the *Express* journalist, named Freedland, recalls the occasion's less spiritual aspects:

We dined together and proceeded to pub and café crawl until the Jew, Indian, Negro, and Malayan had been collected. It was very hard keeping the party going until 6 a.m... It was one of the craziest evenings I have ever spent, and none of the people picked up knew each other.[50]

Crowley's diary is also light on religious significance:

Freedland–& even N∴! acted nobly. We collected the people of the 5 races, took them to the rooms of one Erskine, a terribly dull party, brightening when we got rid of most of them & started whisky. At Cleopatra's Needle Mercury [i.e. Wednesday] 6.22 a.m. I presented the 5 copies and made my magical utterance. And so to bed.

22 Dec. 37. Hangover v. bad.[51]

Distribution gratis of such a grand volume on any larger scale was impossible and at the spring equinox, 21 March 1938, BL8 appeared in sexto-decimo format, paperbound and priced at a shilling. There were two issues, one for England in white paper wrappers, one for America in blue. In this, tractate, form the Law was indeed for all. Crowley was still distributing copies of this edition the year before his death.[52]

II

'My scheme *from the first*,' wrote Crowley to Fra. N∴. about his publishing methods, 'was to create complexity and rarity.'[53] As early as 1907 he considered it was time to unravel some of these complexities and he appended to Volume III of his *Collected Works* (Foyers, 1907) a bibliography of his output to date. He delegated this task to a man superficially totally unqualified in the art of descriptive bibliography, Louis Charles Richard Duncombe Jewell. It is astonishing with what acumen Jewell, rather a sporting type (otter hunter, fisherman), knuckled down to the indoor drudgeries of his task, a science then in its infancy, and the finished product, 'Notes towards an Outline of a Bibliography of the Writings in Prose and Verse of Aleister Crowley,' is a quite unexpected example of bibliographical excellence. Despite its cut-off date of 1905 and its discreet omission of *White Stains*, it is still the most detailed bibliography of Crowley that we possess.[54] In many ways, in his analysis of a book's contents–especial scrutiny being focused on the preliminaries, half-title, title, dedication, imprint–in his attention to binding materials, in his statement of print-runs even when not given in an integral limitation notice, Jewell pioneered techniques that only since the 1950's with the issue of the 'Soho' series of modern bibliographies published by Rupert Hart Davis have become standard practice. Further, by employing an upright rule to denote a line-ending in a title-page transcription as opposed to the double-rule and in the teeth of the (then) doyen of modern bibliographical techniques, T. J. Wise, who favoured the slash, Jewell anticipated a formula that has only recently become *de rigueur*.[55] However, Jewell had neither the space nor, pining for the river-bank, the motivation to elaborate on the reasons for Crowley's choice of materials. This second section will attempt to explore the development of Crowley's tastes in book-design and techniques in marketing the finished product.

Although the man who published Crowley's first book, *Aceldama* (1898), Leonard Charles Smithers–most famous as the publisher of Aubrey Beardsley and Oscar Wilde–wielded considerable influence on Crowley's bibliographical tastes, he had by then met someone else, who most probably effected the introduction, with a keen eye for fine printing: Herbert Charles Pollitt.

Pollitt (1871-1942), who preferred to be called by the Christian name of Jerome, was an amateur dancer with a special preference for transvestism. In his act he used the name of Diane de Rougy, an adaptation of the Parisian dancer's, Liane de Pougy, terpsichorean influences derived, however, not from the Folies-Bergère but from the avant-garde American Loie Fuller, who used electric lights in her show after the manner of the modern laser-beam. Pollitt is the original of *The Babe B. A.,* a Cambridge novel by E. F. Benson (1897) in which, despite decidedly feminine tendencies, he is also credited as being a shrewd observer of a cricket match and as a fearless rugby footballer. Benson also depicts the 'Babe' as an admirer of Aubrey Beardsley, cutting out and framing illustrations from *The Yellow Book* to decorate his room, whereas in fact Pollitt owned several original drawings by Beardsley including some of the *Lysistrata* illustrations published clandestinely by Smithers in 1896. The satirical magazine *The Cambridge A.B.C.* saw more worrying aspects of Pollitt: *'androgyne troublant...ou troublante gynandre'* it states darkly.[56] Crowley was in his second year at Trinity (Pollitt's old college), but the older man despite having already graduated and owning a house in Westmorland continued to reside in the town, apparently for the purposes of picking up undergraduates. Charles Sayle, under-librarian at the University Library (who, curiously, was later to come across Crowley reciting his own poetry in a Snowdonian public-house [57]) and a wry observer of Cambridge *mores*, notes in his diary for 2 February 1897: 'P, with his bad health powerless to get in touch with the younger men.'[58] Pollitt's and Crowley's relationship was undoubtedly a homosexual one and is cryptically alluded to in Crowley's homosexual pastiche *Bagh-I-Muattar, the Scented Garden of Abdullah the Satirist of Shiraz* (Paris and London, 1910[59]), which prints a poem beginning:

Habib hath heard; let all Iran
 who spell aright from A to Z
Exalt thy fame and understand
 with whom I made a marriage-bed

The first letters of the first lines of each stanza of this poem spell out Pollitt's full name (Jerome included), and to underline the liaison the succeeding poem yields, upside-down, the name of Crowley himself.

For some reason Crowley turned against Pollitt, including in his *Collected Works* a vicious attack on him, beginning
 Self-damned, the leprous moisture of thy veins
 Sickens the sunshine.[60]

It is quite possible that Pollitt introduced Crowley to Beardsley: there is a poem in *Aceldama* that suggests Beardsley vouchsafed to Crowley some of his wilder fantasies and there exists a copy of *Aceldama*, one of the two printed on vellum, inscribed by Crowley to Beardsley.[61] Certainly Crowley was familiar with his work and admired it enough to consider adapting one of his designs for a bookplate as their mutual friend, Pollitt, and the artist, Gerald Kelly, had done.[62] He did not, however, divine any occult influences in Beardsley's illustrations. That discovery was left to another occultist, the artist Austin Osman Spare, who was much influenced by Beardsley and several times drew Beardsley's sister, Mabel.[63] Spare was later to become an initiate of Crowley's A∴A∴, taking the magical name of Yihoveaum, but resigned because he could not understand the system.[64] Be that as it may, it was Beardsley's publisher, Leonard Smithers, who next came into Crowley's life and helped him to issue his first two books.

Of all the many curious characters of the 1890's Smithers is one of the most interesting, and certainly one of the shadiest. Born on 19 December 1861, he became a lawyer in Sheffield and in 1891 or 1892 travelled south to London to set up a bookselling and publishing business with an equally disreputable colleague, Harry Sidney Nichols. Alongside *éditions-de-luxe* of the type known in the old days as 'gallant'–court memoirs, Paul de Kock, that sort of thing–was initiated a brisker trade in racier material. Titles include *Gynecocracy, a Narrative of the Misadventures and Psychological Experiences of Julian Robinson (afterwards Viscount Ladywood) under Petticoat Rule* ('Printed for Distribution amongst Private Subscribers Only') and *Teleny, or, The Reverse of the Medal, a Physiological Romance of Today.*[65] Smithers sold Crowley a copy of *Teleny* whose imprint, 'Cosmopoli', although not an original one for books whose place of origin required suppression,[66] he was to copy for his scabrous *Snowdrops from a Curate's Garden*. Inspired by Smithers's publications, Crowley found much amusement at bibliographical bewilderment of this kind. We may cite his use of Shanghai as the place of publication of *Alexandra: a Birthday Ode,* where he also deceives by calling himself 'Ophelia Cox (née Mrs Hunt).'[67]

In 1894 Smithers went into business on his own and for a while was one of the leading publishers of the *fin-de-siècle*. He published Ernest Dowson's *Verses* (1896) and *Pierrot of the Minute* (1897), Pope's *Rape of the Lock* (1896) and Jonson's *Volpone* (1898), all embellished with designs by Beardsley, as well as Beardsley's own *Book of Fifty Drawings* (1897) and *A Second Book of Fifty Drawings* (1899). Throughout 1898 he issued the prestigious illustrated periodical *The Savoy,* again with Beardsley's drawings throughout, which Pollitt had specially bound in vellum.[68] Because of the repercussions of the trial of Oscar Wilde, he was the only publisher willing to risk producing work of a 'decadent' nature. In 1898 he took the logical step of publishing Wilde himself, his poem, *The Ballad of Reading Gaol* and, the next year, his two plays, *The Importance of Being Earnest* and *An Ideal Husband*. However, as Crowley was to experience, Smithers was having problems. The book beautiful–one might add the book questionable–was proving not to be the book marketable. Even when introduced to Crowley in 1897 Smithers was on hard times and he most probably welcomed a young man with a fortune to spend–thirty thousand pounds if Crowley is to be believed–and with manuscripts to be finely printed and published at his own expense.

Aceldama, a Place to Bury Strangers In: a Philosophical Poem by a Gentleman of the University of Cambridge (Shelley, with whom Crowley felt an affinity, had issued works as by 'a gentleman of the university of Oxford') may reflect Crowley's 'talismanic' tastes in that two copies were printed on vellum, but its typography and choice of papers is uniquely Smithers. Ten copies were printed on a paper known as Japanese vellum. Its cost, as a friend of Smithers and later of Crowley's, had written, 'as compared with real vellum is small, and not very much more than the best English handmade rag paper.'[69] Smithers almost invariably issued *éditions de luxe* of Beardsley's books on this paper and it was to remain a firm favourite of Crowley's almost all his life. As we have seen, BL6 and 7 (1936, 1937) were on this paper. Crowley approved, too, of the paper Smithers chose for the ordinary edition–if only eighty-eight copies can be called 'ordinary'–a handmade paper by Abbey Mills, Greenfield. He used it again for *Carmen Saeculare* in 1901 and in a cheaper, machine-made version for *Book Four Part One* (1912).

Altogether Crowley was delighted with his slim effusion. In chivalric vein he inscribed number 16 of the Abbey Mills copies 'To Leonard Smithers from Aleister Crowley, hys fyrst booke'[70] This satisfaction, and the knowledge that Smithers's side-line was the issue of erotica, prompted him in the same year (1898) to entrust him with a manuscript impossible to place elsewhere: *White Stains*. This book of poems, a bird's eye view of the gamut of sexual perversions, required careful handling. Typesetting would have to be done abroad. Smithers commissioned a Dutch firm, Roeloffzen & Hübner for the purpose[71] and took the opportunity of introducing Crowley to another of his favourite papers, Van Gelder handmade. This he had used for the hundred copies of Beardsley's illustrated edition of Aristophanes' *Lysistrata* in 1896 (another clandestine publication) and for Vincent O'Sullivan's *Houses of Sin* (1897). Again, Crowley remembered it with pleasure and used it for *Clouds Without Water* in 1909.[72]

By now Smithers was on the verge of bankruptcy and Crowley's third manuscript, *Green Alps*, another collection of poems, subject-matter an improvement on *White Stains*, suffered accordingly. In quite what form it would have come out is not known because Smithers declared that the sheets had been destroyed in a fire at the printer's. Crowley took the news with admirable stoicism: '(luckily) burnt at the printers and so dropped,' he recorded on p.[93] of the surviving page proofs.[73] It is arguable that, in dire straits, Smithers pocketed Crowley's advance and made the story up but, to be charitable, the Ballantyne Press, a firm known to Crowley (as evidenced by his use of its services in about 1912 to print the twenty-eight page *Manifesto of the M∴M∴M∴*) on 9 December 1899, just about the time printing would have been put in hand, did suffer a disastrous fire at its premises at 9 Essex Street, Strand.[74] It was clear, though, he would have to look elsewhere for someone with the same taste and flair to continue the work Smithers had begun; and he chose a man to whom Smithers had probably already introduced him, the manager of the Chiswick Press, Charles Thomas Jacobi.

To Jacobi until his death in the twenties and to the Press for twenty years after that Crowley offered unstinting loyalty. As he doubtless realized, the standard of its services could hardly be improved on. Founded by Charles Whittingham in 1789 it was for the next fifty years virtually the only English printing works with any pretension whatsoever to typographical felicity; and its publication in 1844 of *So Much of the Diary of Lady Willoughby as Relates to her Domestic History* with its use of the 'old style' faces, was almost solely responsible for the revival of fine printing in this country. Under Jacobi's management in 1890 the press issued a timely reminder of its excellence with the periodical, *The Century Guild Hobby Horse,* and throughout the decade had been yielding an especially rich harvest of typographically distinguished books that drew many authors and publishers to its doors. William Morris used its services in his pre-Kelmscott days;[75] the Bodley Head employed it on a regular basis; and Smithers entrusted it with the production of several of his publications.[76] From 1898 for his third book, *The Tale of Archais,* until 1944 for *The Book of Thoth* Crowley regularly called upon Chiswick to do the printing. It 'had no rival, except Constable's, for excellence of printing,' he records in his *Confessions.*[77]

Not an especial admirer of *art-nouveau,* Crowley was nonetheless drawn to the work of William Morris and the Kelmscott Press and had acquired the Press's masterpiece, the Chaucer of 1896, while still at Cambridge.[78] He admired its simple 'holland-backed' binding and paper label and copied it for *The Tale of Archais* (1898), *Jephthah and Other Mysteries* (1899), *The Mother's Tragedy* [79], *The Soul of Osiris* (1901), and *Tannhäuser* (1902),[80] and to a certain extent for the ten numbers of *The Equinox,* Volume One. He admired, equally, Morris's other Kelmscott binding of vellum with silk ties. That style he employed on some copies of his *Collected Works* 'as being the best protection against the elements. I carried these [three] volumes everywhere, and even when my alleged waterproof rucksack was soaked through, my masterpieces remained intact.'[81] He had an eye, too, for Morris's distinctive archaic typefaces and commissioned from the Chiswick Press two volumes of poetry, *Jezebel and Other Tragic Poems* (1898) and *Ahab and Other Poems* (1903), to be printed in Caxton Antique. With the latter, he was disturbed by the absence, in the fount, of certain punctuation marks: '12pp Ahab have arrived,' he writes to Gerald Kelly. 'The ?, !, -, (), are absurdly modern. Shall I get you to design, and have cast, proper types, or shall I use full stops only (to the prejudice of the reader) and replace the dash and brackets by the hyphen mark [?].'[82]

Typographical infelicities continued to disturb Crowley later on. In his diary for 1924 he rails against Jane Wolfe, 'Soror Estai', whom he had requested to oversee the production of *Songs for Italy* [83]:

I can never see or write to her again.[84] What adds to the horror is that she did it with such very good intentions and took such pains and made such sacrifices–and all to blot my fame indelibly with the abomination of vile printing.[85]

In contradistinction to typographical scrupulousness is his quite astonishing uninterest in proof-correcting. Literals abound in his books; from their pages errata slips flutter like autumn leaves. 'Proof-reading', he wrote to Fra. N∴, 'is an art which I strongly recommend you not to learn; as long as there are any sewers to clean, you would be ill-advised to adopt it as a profession.'[86] Nonetheless, he must have been upset that the coloured plate of the funerary tablet of Ankh-f-n-khonsu that adorned BL6 and BL7 was miscaptioned, and he angrily annotated the passage of Chinese in *Konx Om Pax*: 'Upside down. Damn Jacoby.'[87] Even after his death–analogy here with A. E. Housman, who unlike Crowley dreaded and despised misprints–he was pursued by printers' devils and his birth date is misprinted, October 18th for October 12th, on the order of his funeral service.'[88]

Smithers went bankrupt in 1899, yet Smithers bankrupt continued to operate much as Smithers in funds: piracies, clandestine ruderies, reliance on the marketability of anything illustrated by Beardsley. Crowley, however, parted company with him. There may after all have been a row about what actually happened to *Green Alps*. Certainly Crowley revised his opinion about the burning of the book's being 'lucky', liking some of the lost poems well enough to publish them in *Oracles* (1905). When Duncombe-Jewell came to record details concerning *Aceldama*, Crowley informed him not that it had been produced by the publisher of Oscar Wilde and Ernest Dowson and Aubrey Beardsley but 'by an obscure printer in the Brompton-road.' He needed therefore to find another firm which could not only print but, because his output was annually increasing, could warehouse, market, and distribute this rising output. He chose the well-established company of Kegan Paul, Trench, Trübner. Quite why, we do not know. Perhaps because it published books on Oriental languages, which interested Crowley a good deal; perhaps because ever since its association with Tennyson it had been keen to publish, though not necessarily at its own expense, the work of contemporary poets. Furthermore, the printing bill footed, Kegan Paul did not much care what their authors wrote about. (The most notorious Kegan Paul author, the Revd Edwin Emmanuel Bradford, between 1908 and 1930, paid for twelve volumes of cheery but flagrantly pedophilic poetry without anyone at Kegan Paul's turning a hair.) Kegan Paul distributed *The Tale of Archais* and *Songs of the Spirit* (1898), *An Appeal to the American Republic* (1899), *The Soul of Osiris* and *Carmen Saeculare* (1901)[89] and *Tannhäuser* (1902). On board ship for Cairo and Rangoon with his new bride, Rose Kelly, Crowley wrote to Kegan Paul's manager, Spencer C. Blackett, to arrange publication of his play *The Argonauts*. Already set up by Chiswick, it needed only a title-page bearing Kegan Paul's imprint.[90] Blackett may have taken the opportunity to consult the sales ledger to see how Crowley's other books were faring. He would have been appalled by what he saw. Despite deluging the press with no fewer than eighty-two review copies, only ten copies of *Jephthah and Other Mysteries* had been sold.[91] *Tannhäuser*, too, had managed only ten; and of the five hundred copies of *An Appeal to the American Republic* and *The Mother's Tragedy* there had been no sale whatsoever.

Apprised of the situation, Crowley decided to try marketing his books himself and with *The Argonauts* (1904) founded the Society for the Propagation of Religious Truth (a deliberate mimicry of the two hundred-year-old Church of England publishing firm, the Society for Promoting Christian Knowledge), its headquarters his shooting lodge, Boleskine, Foyers, Inverness, and took over from Kegan Paul its unsold stocks. In some cases, *Tannhäuser* and *A Mother's Tragedy*, he cancelled Kegan Paul title-leaves and inserted S.P.R.T. ones; others he left as they were; new books were given the new imprint. Society titles usually have a catalogue of available books bound in the back, sometimes headed 'The Works of Mr Aleister Crowley,' sometimes, less attractively, 'The Excreta of Aleister Crowley.' Titles, as a general rule, moved fairly slowly. Crowley would not, never did, regard them as remainders. Like his better-selling contemporary, John Drinkwater, he preferred to consider them as 'engaging little packets of duplicates,'[93] values increasing rather than depreciating with the passing of time. Indeed, he was in the habit of offering them or dumping them on creditors, landlords and the like, in lieu of cash, the recipients finding disposal tricky and for the most part unrewarding. As late as July 1964, Sotheby's auctioned such a cache and–the 'hippie' movement that would refloat Crowley on the antiquarian market being not yet under way–hammer prices were poor. A few years later things would be different. There would be a 'hippie' version of *The Book of the Law*[94] and the rock-'n'-rollers associated with the drug culture would take Crowley to their bosoms. The Beatles included his picture in the photomontage of the famous and infamous (Beardsley included) who adorned the sleeve of their album, *Sergeant Pepper's Lonely Hearts Club Band* (1967). Jimmy Page, lead guitarist of Led Zeppelin, another English band, proclaimed his allegiance to the Law of Thelema by incising the run-off matrix of its third album, *Led Zeppelin III*, with the words 'Do What Thou Wilt.'[95] One of the better American psychedelic bands called itself The Golden Dawn[96] and Van Morrison, the Irish singer, inspired perhaps more by W. B. Yeats than by Crowley, refers to the Golden Dawn in a recording as recent as 1983.[97] The 'king' of rock-'n'-rollers, Elvis Presley, tinkered vaguely with the irrational. It is noteworthy that, among the many floral tributes on his grave at the first anniversary of his death, there was placed a wreath of curious design bearing a remarkable resemblance to the Rose Cross of the Order of the Golden Dawn.[98]

It is hard to explain, when Crowley was so satisfied with Chiswick's work, why, in 1904, he sought out a French printer, Philippe Renouard, 19 rue des Saints-Pères, Paris, to print some of his work. Probably the explanation is that he had a book or two on the stocks Chiswick would in no circumstances have handled and, at the same time, that he wished to set Renouard at his ease by offering him non-erotic works as well as distinctly disturbing ones. On the first title, *The Sword of Song* ('Benares', 1904) Renouard was happy to place his imprint, not noticing, presumably, that the initial letters of some of the hanging notes in the appendix, 'Ambrosii Magi Hortus Rosarum,' spelled out four-letter words of a fairly basic nature. They passed muster, too, when Turnbull & Spears of Edinburgh came to reprint the appendix in *Collected Works*, but they were exposed in 1911 during a libel-suit brought by a colleague, George Cecil Jones, against a scandal-sheet called *The Looking Glass*. Crowley did not give evidence but, in a fanciful account of the proceedings he had printed under the pseudonym of Leo Vincey, feigned surprise and declared that the formations were coincidental. By the same token, he wrote, the judge's name (Scrutton) was the 'anagram of a sentence–not merely a word, mark you!–which asserts a pathological fact familiar to every Syphilographer and his clients, couched in the crudest and coarsest language!'[99] Just as he enjoyed using bewildering place-names on his books, Crowley enjoyed too cryptogrammatical indecencies of this sort. Compositors at the Arden Press, Letchworth, could hardly be expected to work out, while setting *Amphora* [1909], 'privately printed for the Authoress and her

Intimates,' that the couplet formed by reading the first letter of the first word and the first letter of the last word in the 'Epilogue' read 'The Virgin Mary I desire / But arseholes set my prick on fire.' The joke was not over, for although he took out the Epilogue when he offered them the book, he managed to persuade the Roman Catholic publishers, Burns & Oates, of the poems' theological orthodoxy and of the actual existence of their saintly authoress. Lesbian undertones (Crowley inscribed a copy 'To darling Gretchen in memory of happy convent days from Phyllis Dare' to underline the point) also went unrecognized, but eventually Burns & Oates discovered the author's true identity and returned the unsold sheets to Crowley.[100]

The second book, *Snowdrops from a Curate's Garden* ('1881 A.D., Cosmopoli, imprimé sous le manteau et ne se vend nulle part'), a collection of erotic prose and verse Crowley claimed to have distributed 'to people I despised for their piggish lust–to cure them by surfeit,'[101] Renouard did not care to sign; but his use on *The Sword of Song* and on *Snowdrops* of similar vignettes both signed 'L. M.' and his practice, not uncommon on the continent, of using capital letters when paginating in Roman numerals, lay *Snowdrops* squarely at Renouard's door.[102]

Typographically Crowley was well pleased with him, believing him good enough to teach even the Chiswick Press a few tricks. He passed to Jacobi a copy of Renouard's printing of *Rosa Mundi* and bade him follow the Frenchman's house style for the companion volumes, *Rosa Coeli* and *Rosa Inferni* (1907).[103] Renouard reminded Crowley of the tastefulness of grey 'china' paper, the very opposite of the yellow 'japanese' one he already favoured–soft, fibrous, lightweight, rough-surfaced, as opposed to hard, shiny, heavy–which the French regularly employed for *éditions-de-luxe* and which Crowley himself had used to print his first ever essay on magic, *Berashith*.[104] Ten copies of the three 'Rosa' poems and of *Rodin in Rime* (1907) are found on that material.

Another 'suspect' book entrusted to Renouard, *Bagh-I-Muattar, the Scented Garden of Abdullah the Satirist of Shiraz* (in which, as we have seen, Crowley confesses to his love-affair with Pollitt), suffered a fate to which all such publications are from time to time prone. In 1924, twelve cases of Crowley's books addressed to his disciple Norman Mudd and shipped aboard *SS Svein Jarl* were seized under Section 42 of the Customs Consolidation Act, 1876.[105] Among them were thirty-two copies of Renouard's *Bagh*. All were destroyed.[106]

Renouard printed two other books with erotic undertones. *Clouds Without Water*, 'privately printed for circulation among ministers of religion,' on one of Crowley's favourite papers, Van Gelder, contains acrostic references to 'Lola', 'one of the most exquisitely beautiful young girls, by

English standards, that ever breathed or blushed,'[107] and to a sculptress studying under Rodin who introduced Crowley to 'the torturing pleasures of algolagny on the spiritual plane.' Lola's name (her real one was Vera) can be discovered in the first four letters of the first four lines on pages 3, 19, 35, 67, and 117; the sculptress's, Kathleen Bruce, in the first letters of the lines of the 'Terzain' on page XXI (note Renouard's capitalization). By ill-chance her husband, the famous explorer Robert Falcon Scot, was informed of the cryptogram by a rival for her affections. 'As a matter of fact', Crowley wrote tersely, 'it was a simple one; he had merely to take a rule and draw a straight line to make the name and surname of the girl stand out *en toutes lettres*...It might seem that such a man would not know how to draw a line anywhere but he drew this.'[108]

The World's Tragedy, 'privately printed for circulation in free countries; copies must not be imported into England or America,' Renouard got out the following year, 1910, again on Crowley's favourite Van Gelder. The preface contains revelatory passages about homosexual practices in English schools in general and among Crowley's family in particular. He wrote to the distinguished book-collector John Quinn (who owned, among other treasures, the manuscript of James Joyce's *Ulysses*): 'World's Tragedy. 100 printed. All mutilated of pp xxvii and xxviii [i.e. the homosexual references] except in a few copies in the hands of the author's friends.'[109] Quinn came as a windfall to Crowley–at least, a windfall after a magical operation to acquire wealth–although he spent between seven and eight hundred dollars against Crowley's expectation of three or four thousand.[110] He bought sixty-seven items, virtually a complete collection of Crowley's output to 1914, and the manuscripts of *A Mother's Tragedy, Alice: An Adultery, The Soul of Osiris,* and 'The King of Terror' (printed under the title of 'The Testament of Magdalen Blair' in *The Equinox* for March 1913).[111]

For some reason, one book entrusted to Renouard never saw the light of day at all:

Alexandra, a Birthday Ode suggested by Abbey's Masterpiece in the Academy of 1904 being the Watkin Tower of English Literature (vice Kubla Khan and Hyperion retired hurt), the Unfinished or Mulitated [*sic*] (or both) Manuscript or [*sic*] Mr Alfred Austin, Mr Owen Seaman, or Mr A. N. Other rescued from the flames and copied fair, transcribed, edited, annotated, arranged, printed, published by Ophelia Cor [*sic*] (née McHunt) [*sic*] and Diaper of the Woman's Monthly. Shanghai 1905. Five Dollars.

Gerald Yorke in his bibliography appended to John Symonds's life of Crowley, *The Great Beast* (1951), suggests the whole stock was 'destroyed by H.M. Customs on the grounds of obscenity and *lèse-majesté*,' but since Renouard's two other suspect books, *Snowdrops* and *Bagh-I-Muattar*, get into circulation, albeit in a handful of copies, one wonders if this supposition is correct.[112]

After a brief liaison with a London publisher, Wieland & Co., who published between 1911 and 1913 *The High History of Sir Palamedes, Mortadello: the Angel of Venice,* the first two parts of *Book Four,* Crowley's Baudelaire translations, *Little Poems in Prose,* and No. 9 of Vol. One of *The Equinox,* Crowley departed for the United States. Not much got done over there: an abortive volume of verse, *The Giant's Thumb* (New York, Mitchell Kennerley, 1915), only reached the proof-stage;[113] Vol. III, No. 1 of *The Equinox* (the 'Blue' Equinox) came out in Detroit.

In 1920, after a brief return to England, Crowley founded at Cefalù, Sicily, the Abbey of Thelema whence, after his expulsion by Mussolini in 1923, he became itinerant. Whereas before it had amused him to put outlandish place-names on his title-pages (Benares for *The Sword of Song,* Shanghai for *Alexandra,* Pallanza for *Household Gods*) to enhance his ideas of 'complexity and rarity', now he was forced to do so. As well as BL4, he issued from Tunis four pamphlets, *Songs For Italy,* (1923), *The World Teacher to the Theosophical Society, The Avenger to the Theosophical Society,* and *Madame Tussaud-Besant* (1925). Two further broadsheets came out at Weida in 1925, one more from Leipzig. The second issue of Wieland's *Little Poems in Prose* was issued in Paris, where he took up residence in 1928. Had he not been expelled from France in 1929 *Magick* might also have appeared there.

In 1930 he returned to England. Owing to a smear campaign by the newspapers he was not exactly popular there and he circulated a pamphlet, *An Open Letter to Lord Beaverbrook,* to try and clear his name, and engaged a highly-placed police official to test the domestic temperature. His disciple, Fra. N.·., was set to work to establish a London headquarters to distribute several books then on the stocks: his novel, *Moonchild*; the seven volumes of his Confessions or 'autohagiography', as he called it,[114] the three thousand copies of the Parisian-printed *Magick in Theory and Practice,* and of course an 'ideal' edition of *The Book of the Law.*

At first Crowley considered buying a private press. Many had sprung up in the wake of Francis Meynell's successful venture, the Nonesuch: Haslewood Books (1924), Fortune (1925), Fanfrolico (1926), Scholartis and Cresset (1927), Haymarket (1928), Aquila (1929). There is circumstantial evidence to suggest a flirtation with the Fortune Press or at least consultations about marketing with the press's enigmatic director, Reginald Ashley Caton (for whom see pp47-62). Crowley engaged one of Fortune's illustrators, Beresford Egan, to design the dust-jacket of *Moonchild* and another, Jean de Bosschère, to embellish the unsold copies of Wieland's *Little Poems in Prose* with the insertion of new copperplate engravings. Caton was to do the selfsame thing for the slow-moving unillustrated *Songs of Bilitis* by Pierre Louÿs.[115] Montague Summers, the authority on witchcraft and friend of Crowley despite divergent viewpoints, might have been the intermediary in the negotiations. His eye then turned on Aquila. Founded by James Cleugh, Frederick Hallis, and Alex Keiller, it employed Caslon old face types which Crowley would have often seen when visiting Jacobi at Chiswick and had issued in 1929 a fine edition of Marlowe's *Edward the Second* with the heraldic shields of the characters in the play so splendidly emblazoned in gold and colours that they could have reminded Crowley of the Golden Dawn badges and lamens.[116] This plan, however, came to nothing.

The Fanfrolico Press, however, had as manager a man who appealed to Crowley and whose Nietzschean philosophy–salted with something of the idealism of Yeats' *A Vision*–was not unsympathetic to his aims: Percival Reginald Stephensen. Fanfrolico had been started by an Australian, Jack Lindsay, and had printed a distinguished edition of Aristophanes' *Lysistrata* with illustrations by Jack's father, Norman.[117] With that and with its magazine, *The London Aphrodite*, it was deliberately taunting 'the Squirearchy and the self-appointed guardians of public morals,'[118] to which Stephensen added fuel by writing *The Sink of Solitude,* a squib on Radclyffe Hall's *Well Of Loneliness.* Increasingly disquieted by his manager's fencing with the Establishment and by the fact he was planning to bring out a book of D. H. Lawrence's paintings and the definitive (by which Stephensen meant unexpurgated) edition of his poems, *Pansies,* Lindsay persuaded him to launch a breakaway press, the Mandrake, for those purposes. Money, however, was at a premium. For interim capital it drew on a bookseller, Edward Goldston; and Stephensen–whose continuing warmth to Crowley's ideals prompted him to collaborate in a lengthy apologia, *The Legend of Aleister Crowley,* a sort of extended *Open Letter to Lord Beaverbrook*–was happy to accept a thousand pounds from Fra. N∴ and another thousand from Crowley's German disciple, Karl Germer (Fra.Saturnus) in return for directorships. With this substantial foot in Mandrake's door Crowley delivered the manuscript of *Moonchild* and the multi-volume *Confessions.*

Stephensen must have worked hard. By 1930 he had in print both the Lawrence books; 2,500 copies of *Moonchild*; a book of Crowley's short stories, *The Stratagem*; eight hundred copies of each of the first two volumes of *The Confessions* and the third volume in proof; his own *Legend*; and he had taken delivery of, had had bound–in four wrappered parts and, for subscribers, in one cloth-bound volume–the 3,000 copies of *Magick in Theory and Practice.* Another book of Crowley's short stories, *Golden Twigs,* and a collection of a hundred of his poems were also in the pipeline.

D. H. Lawrence had it that Mandrake collapsed: 'Oh that Mandrake', he wrote towards the end of his life, 'vegetable of ill omen.'[119] But Stephensen does not put it quite like that:

> The Mandrake Press did not 'lose money'. It wound up partly because Goldston could shrewdly anticipate that the effects of the 'Depression' in 1930 would be adverse to Limited Editions, and partly because our star author, Aleister Crowley, was so difficult to handle that Goldston and I sold our interests to three [120] of Crowley's nominees, who carried it on for a while then wound it up.[121]

At this point Fra. N∴ withdrew both his money and his allegiance and embraced the rather longer-established creed of Buddhism. Crowley fought on as best he could. We have seen how he produced BL6 and 7 with financial help from Pearl Brookesmith. There were problems other than financial. BL6's distributors, Simpkin Marshall, threatened to pull out, so the British Monomark Corporation was engaged to supply a box-number, 'BCM/ANKH', to which orders, trade and retail, could be sent. From this address was also issued *The Heart of the Master* (1938). Crowley recalled that Leonard Smithers had issued one of his 'miniature' editions of *The Rape of the Lock* in a limp suede binding, and he had eleven copies bound in that material.[122] He allowed himself, as well, another of his 'visual' jokes. In 1914 he had published a suspect poem, *Chicago May* (fifty copies on Whatman handmade paper and three on vellum: 'the possessor...is earnestly requested to retain the same under lock and key, and in no wise to part with it until the year 1964'), that had resembled a number of *The English Review* to which he was then contributing. Now, at the winter solstice of 1939, he issued *Temperance, a Tract for the Times*, a collection of rowdy drinking-songs dedicated to the teetotal Lady Astor. It was bound like the elaborate wine-list of a grand restaurant or transatlantic liner, its disjunct leaves caught with a knotted gold cord.

As can be imagined, he was no mean publicist. Earlier on prospectuses for his books had combined the blandishments of sales patter with cool commonsense. 'Unique opportunity', blared one of the prospectuses for *Why Jesus Wept*: 'Order early to avoid Armageddon.' 'Look slippy, boys!' urged another. 'Christ may come at any moment. He won't like it if you haven't read the book...' Below was printed a thoroughly practical order form: 'Dear Poet, Please send me...cop...of this at once. I enclose the cash.' Even in 1942 techniques had not been forgotten. The deliberately misprinted blurb on the prospectus for *The Fun of the Fair* reads: 'the book will be as expensive and nice as this prospectus is cheap and nasty.' After the university authorities had forbidden him to deliver his lecture on Gilles de Rais and he had decided to have it printed and rushed to Oxford for distribution among the students, he wrote to Arthur Calder-Marshall, president of the Poetry Society who had invited him to talk: 'Please make arrangements to have Sandwich men on the streets to sell *The Banned Lecture*.'[123]

For quite a while Crowley had been unable to afford the services of his beloved Chiswick Press. He had used 'W.P.S.' (Western Printing Services, the firm who had set BL6 and 7) for *Khing Kang King, Eight Lectures on Yoga,* and *England Stand Fast,* 'Botolph' Printing Works for *The Banned Lecture* ('at an hour's notice'),[124] 'Apex' Printing Services for *Temperance.* Now with the Second World War, into which, by successive publications of *The Book of the Law,* the Western world had been inexorably plunged, he returned to them for *Thumbs Up,* a poem to aid the war-effort. Its talismanic publication date, 'An Ixv Sol in 0°0'0" Leo, 6.26 a.m. July 23, 1941 e.v.,' he put forward until 11 August so that it should include a frontispiece portrait.[125] In common with BL8 there was a cheap edition 'for free distribution among the soldiers and workers of the forces of freedom.'

He had one more shot in his locker, a book in every way as important as *Magick* or *The Book of the Law,* a treatise on the Tarot cards he called *The Book of Thoth.* Here again Golden Dawn roots were exposed, for although he overlaid the system with his own, Thelemic, ideas, changing the order of two of the Trumps in accordance with Aiwaz's commands, the greater part of its teachings can be found in the Golden Dawn's 'Book T.'[126] Chiswick was able to produce a stock of Arnold unbleached handmade paper which neatly side-stepped Board of Trade restrictions on the use and quality of paper for new books. The binding, russet half-morocco with raised bands and sides of a striking Egyptian-patterned paper,[127] was entrusted to the old established London firm of Sangorski & Sutcliffe who, in palmier days, had specially bound fine-paper copies of his own books for his personal library.[128] The book was embellished with coloured and black-and-white plates of newly designed cards by Lady Frieda Harris. A typically elaborate prospectus narrowly escaped contravening another of what Crowley called 'those fool regulations'[129] which forbade the circulation of leaflets advertising new books; but a loophole was found at the last moment: *The Book of Thoth* constituted Vol. III, No. 5 of *The Equinox,* a periodical publication, and magazines were not subject to the control.

After Crowley's death in 1947 the Thelema Publishing Company in America, Karl Germer's organization, published *Liber Aleph,* which he had considered as important a book as any, and *Magick without Tears,* a spirited and lucid treatise on magic written in epistolary form.[130] Pirates then got to work, popping rare morsels under their photostatic grills and serving them up blurred, shoddy, photolithographically etiolated, and in contravention both of earthly copyright and of Aiwaz's extraterrestrial requirements. Three publications would, however, have found favour. Two came from the 'Dove' Press,[131] *Atlantis*, a prose work published to coincide with the vernal equinox of 1970 in an edition of a thousand copies, and a broadsheet poem, *Hymn to Lucifer*, that appeared at the summer solstice of the same year. The former has twenty-two special copies embellished with ribbons and seals and with eight symbolic illustrations by the Russian artist Nicolas Kalmakoff. Of the latter, six numbered copies were ensplendoured with seals and ribbons and, more importantly, a talismanic sigil. This sigil is traced not in ink but 'in two sacramental substances'. In 1955 Fra.N∴ issued a revised edition of *777* with the Neptune Press, London, for which he drew on his own considerable store of occult learning, at the same time–in recollection of his friend's ideals of 'complexity and rarity'–enjoying an elaborate bibliographical joke. Two deluxe issues were available, both on handmade paper, the first limited to twelve copies bound in crimson vellum, the second to seven copies in blue morocco containing an unpublished poem by Crowley. What neither prospectus nor limitation notice stated was that each of the seven copies contains a *different* poem.[132]

2
Montague Summers*

THE name of Montague Summers, its dactyl and spondee tripping lightly, almost wickedly across the tongue, seems to personify that blend of eroticism and religion which, however reprehensible, provokes–like the Abbé Boullan, Aleister Crowley and the subject of our last talk, Theodore Reuss–a perennial fascination in the minds of students of the human psyche. Facts about his life are muddied by speculation. Rumours blur discernible outlines. The picture will probably always remain unclear. Let us see if we can uncover, though, a fragment of the original canvas.

His obsession with erotica he hardly bothered to suppress. Admittedly few knew that among the books found on his death was a treasured copy of *Fanny Hill*–a novel from a literary period he did not much admire–discreetly labelled *Odes of Spring* and a portfolio of watercolours of guardsmen engaged in pursuits which only the confines of their sentry-box saved from the somatically impossible. Publicly, however, or at least 'for Adult Students of Social Questions', he issued in 1920 the first treatise in English on the Marquis de Sade. Thirteen years later, prefaced by an attack on the very anti-clerical literature he was resurrecting, he published a translation of *The Confessions of Madeleine Bavent,* the genre's most pernicious example. His passion for the drama of the Restoration was not unaligned to its indecencies. A conversation with a publisher is reported. Summers opened proceedings in a cheerful voice: 'I have discovered some hitherto unknown couplets which are, regrettably, very indecent.' The voice changed to one of the darkest

---

* This talk, shorn only of interpolations, frivolous for the most part, was given to The Society on 16 March 1984. The Society is a society in London. In accordance with occult precepts it requires no further advertisement.

gloom: 'Fortunately in the original text the most opprobrious words are indicated by dashes...*but*' (the mood changing again to one of excellent humour) 'I regret infinitely to report that these words always come at the end of lines and therefore' (with a jolly chuckle) 'the rhyme unfortunately indicates the missing word.' Here are some lines from his first book, *Antinous and Other Poems*, printed at his own expense by Sisley's, 'Makers of Beautiful Books' :

> Upon the café deewan, gaily shawled,
>> There lies a lad whose lips gleam sherbet-wet
> From time to time his olive face is palled
>> By the blue fume of a dull cigarette.

None of this matters very much. Sexual unorthodoxy, whether in sentry-boxes or not, seems harmless enough given the compliance of the parties involved but in the same book is another poem, 'To a Dead Acolyte': Here ground grows more treacherous.

> Thy lips are still and pale,
> Pale from Death's icy kiss.
> The radiance of thine wondrous eyes
> No more shall flame with earthly bliss.
> No more thy reverent accents, sweet,
> Shall answer at the Mass,
> No more thy gentle flower-like feet
> About the Altar pass.

And what sort of ceremony, we must ask ourselves, is here in progress?

> Clad in Love's priests' apparel,
> White alb and scarlet camail,
> We stand in his dim carrell
>> With prayer and ritual meet.
> We wave the fragrant censer,
> And as the fume steams denser,
> The Gloria groweth tenser,
>> That mounts unto his feet.

> Across the crowded palace
> His bright eyes gleam with malice,
> When we uplift the chalice,
>> Brimful of sanguine wine.
> No mass more sweet than this is,
> A liturgy of kisses,
> What time the metheglin hisses
>> Plashed o'er the fumid shrine.

38

He dreams of bygone pleasures,
Whose passion kenned no measures,
Of all his secret treasures,
    The lust of long dead men.
And thro' dishevelled tresses,
He smiles at our caresses,
To know that he possesses
    As great power now as then.

This is satanism, satanism celebrated by Montague Summers in 1907 with as much fervour as in 1926 he would denounce it in his *History of Witchcraft and Demonology*:

> I have endeavoured to show the witch as she really was–an evil liver, a social pest and parasite; the devotee of a loathly and obscene creed; an adept at poisoning, blackmail and other creeping crimes; a member of a powerful secret organization inimicable to Church and State; a blasphemer in word and deed...battening upon the filth and foulest passions of the age.

Oh, yes. People grow up. They commit *voltes-faces*. They regret past indiscretions. They cover youthful tracks. In Summers's case this is not the whole truth.

At this point, I ought to present a brief sketch of Summers's life.

He was born at Clifton into a rich middle-class family in 1880. Sent to Clifton College, he, at fifteen, exhibited first signs of reconditeness and erudition by being the only boy in the form who knew the rules of ombre, the card-game described in *The Rape of the Lock*. His father, a JP, kept a good library. He was, though, a stern censor of reading matter. A few books, as Summers lovingly, too lovingly, dwells on in his rather dull autobiography, were kept locked up. Juvenile inquisitiveness was to become an adult obsession. The other day, while preparing this talk, I lit upon a volume of tracts for the young. Nestling between articles such as 'In His Spare Moments' and 'How Boys Bathe in Finland', I came across one on the dangers of 'literature.' In dialogue form, it could well be a conversation between the youthful Summers and his father:

> 'Papa', said Arthur Wilson one evening, 'will you give me the key of the bookcase in your study?'
> 'Why, my boy?'
> 'I wish to take out a book.'
> 'Which book?'
> 'A book from the high shelf.'
> 'That is not answering my question.'
> 'A scarlet book, papa...Was it you, papa, who locked it up?'
> 'Yes.'

'Why did you do so?'
'Because I did not wish you to read it. I have not read it myself but I know the name of the writer well. He is a Frenchman.'

Summers went to Trinity College, Oxford. By this time things were going seriously awry. Summers's father could well have echoed Kipling's (though not of course with the cockney accent):

Clifton and Trinity College. I ought to ha' sent you to sea
But I stood you an education, an' what have you done for me?
The things I knew was proper you wouldn't thank me to give,
And the things I knew was rotten you said was the way to live.
For you muddled with books and pictures, and china an' etchin's and fans
And your rooms in College were beastly—more like a whore's than a man's.

Summers was bitterly to regret his muddling with books and pictures and the poor degree it resulted in. At this time he was being lured by the Roman Church, at any rate by her outward trappings. However, he entered the Anglican theological college at Lichfield and took deacon's orders in 1908, the year after he issued the revealing poems we have just heard. He was appointed to a curacy in Bath and then one in the Bristol suburb of Bitton under an eccentric and elderly vicar, Canon Ellacombe. By this time he was in a thoroughly neurotic state. The curacy terminated when Summers was arraigned on a charge of paederasty. Nobody, even the good canon if ever he was apprised of it, should have been surprised.

Summers was acquitted. The next year he embraced the Roman faith. We are now sailing into the choppy waters of Summers's orders and I do not propose to take you very deeply upon them. The whole question, the 'vexed' question as Summers would have put it, is dealt with by his biographer, himself a priest. Suffice it to say that Summers was a good theologian. Orders even if schismatically conferred or, another possibility, obtained abroad, would have, for him, to have been valid. Fr Ronald Knox, whose antipathy to Summers was matched only by Summers's to him, was convinced he was correctly in orders. Knox, who doesn't always seem to have been the bright spark he's cracked up to be, refused to appear between the same covers as Summers in an anthology of Catholic biographies. The editor of this volume, the Revd Claude Williamson, whom I knew well, was also certain that Summers was a priest. Williamson exhibited eccentricities every bit as strange as Summers's. He drew a stipend from the Anglican, swore allegiance to the Roman faith. There were stories of unfrocking, a ban at least on his celebrating mass in this country. He inhabited the basement and ground floor of a seedy rooming-house in the same London street where, in petulant mood, Rimbaud had roomed with Verlaine. The main room was packed with bookshelves from floor to ceiling, not only against the walls but across the whole floor-space, the occasional cranny occupied by a stick or two of furniture and a ponderous escritoire.

There were two peculiarities about these books, found on examination to juxtapose religion, sex, and magic in much the same way as they were juxtaposed in Summers's mind. With few exceptions they had been nicked. Indication of content had been rendered difficult by the positioning between their spines and the protective glass of the cases of a series of faded photographs. All were of boys. Along their ranks, when Claude got to know you better, he enjoyed a guided tour pointing out among the mortar-boards and knickerbockers who in his opinion had been 'hot stuff.' Another indication, if one were needed, of Claude's tastes in that direction lay in his weekly visit to Westminster swimming baths. This was not for exercise but for the purpose of obtaining a clean teatowel. Some time before, he had become possessed (probably by the same method he had acquired the bulk of his library) of a towel, hireable at the baths by those who had omitted to bring their own and intended to be placed in a laundry basket at the bath's exit when it had served its turn. This he had discovered had come in handy for drying up purposes and required, as I have said, a weekly change. Claude would secrete the dirty towel about his person and from the darkness of his cubicle bide his time until some unsuspecting lad had completed his dip and consigned his towel to the recesses of the laundry-basket. Then with a dexterity not evident in other activities–he was a heavy, lumbering man getting on in years–Claude would hurry to the basket, whip from his pocket his gravy-stained offering and substitute for it the damp, faintly aromatic, bundle which he would bear off to his basement for its humble stint at his draining-board. Despite these admissions of unorthodoxy, which if you were young enough he would supplement with a grueling chase around his sofa, he would never believe that Summers shared his tastes and I am telling you all this not in a vein of prurient reminiscence but to prove how very carefully even from a sympathetic soul Summers would guard all hints of personal involvement. We are dealing very likely with a deeply divided personality.

From 1913, then, Summers called himself a priest. Short of money, despite a legacy from his father which the old man had cannily entrammelled in a complicated trust, Summers took up school-mastering. He found it a tiring and unrewarding task. Around this time his boyhood fascination for old plays, many of which he performed on his toy theatre or as he preferred to call it, his juvenile stage, began to bear fruit. He published his first two editions of Restoration dramatists, Buckingham's *Rehearsal,* the play that satirizes all its contemporaries, and a six-volume set of Aphra Behn. It is in this realm of scholarship that Summers showed himself as no dry-as-dust academic, for he began to revive on the stage as well this exceedingly rich vein of our dramatic heritage that since Scott had edited Dryden (Summers said very badly) had been considered unreadable and unwatchable. Summers became a producer, his strange bat-like figure remarked on by London theatre-going society. The importance of these productions, in which many actors and actresses later to become famous appeared–Sybil Thorndike, Athene Seyler, Edith Evans, Baliol Holloway, Ernest Thesiger–can hardly be over-emphasized. By all accounts they were splendid. In one of these plays, in no more than a walk-on part, appeared a young actor. His name was Anatole James. He was a man Summers was later to shun. We shall soon see why.

But The Phoenix–as this repertory was called–was not the only society in which Summers from 1918 to 1923 played a leading role. At about the time London observed him beaming from his box in his clerical robes, in dingier surroundings another society gathered in secret: the British Society for the Study of Sex Psychology.

The B.S.S.S.P. was little more than a cabal of homosexuals. Laurence Housman was a member, Edward Carpenter, Havelock Ellis, young Anatole James. Sometimes, however, lectures were given on other aspects. These did not go down so well. Marie Stopes one evening gave a talk on birth control. It was of some length. At last time came for questions. None was forthcoming. The silence became awkward. Miss Stopes's eyes vainly raked the audience for signs of life. Eventually at the back of the hall a Scotsman rose to his feet. He addressed the meeting in rounded tones: 'Is the Society aware that in Pairsia, sodomy is no' a crime?'

I suspect it was at one of the B.S.S.S.P. meetings–not likely the one on birth control–that Summers met C.K.Ogden, general editor of the 'History of Civilization' series for Kegan Paul and that one of Summers' talks–he gave several, only the one on the Marquis de Sade being printed–suggested to Ogden he would be the man to write the two volumes on witchcraft the series required. They appeared in 1926 and 1927 and after that Summers was retained to write out-of-series works on the vampire and the werewolf.

Summers's literary plate was beginning to fill up. Two further figures now had their eye on him. In 1923, after internal squabbles had divided The Phoenix and Summers had resigned, a young typographer, Francis Meynell, founded the Nonesuch Press, its aims being to provide finely printed books at fair prices. This was an original idea. The revival of fine printing by William Morris at the Kelmscott and St John Hornby at the Ashendene Press was doubtless Meynell's jumping-off point, but he recognized that their books were too expensive and despite their often-repeated canons for fine printing as often as not illegible. Meynell wanted to retain the collectable virtues of those presses by limiting his editions though not so drastically, in the expectation, which was amply fulfilled, not only of collectors snapping them up as a possible return on their money, but because of the literary importance of the texts they presented. He therefore engaged Summers for the definitive editions of the plays of William Congreve, William Wycherley, Thomas Otway and John Dryden.

Meynell's activities were being closely observed by a man in every way as odd as any we have so far mentioned. Tall, infinitely reclusive, Reginald Ashley Caton was, at the time we are talking of, advertisement manager for a tobacco trade journal. He had ambitions to be a publisher. He did not see why he should not do as well as Nonesuch. To achieve this end he did a very simple thing. He pinched three of their books and reprinted them under his own imprint, The Fortune Press. In excuse it could be said he made editorial changes in texts already out of copyright, but they were typographically indistinguishable. Until then there had been no test case for infringement of typographical copyright. There was now to be one. Meynell won and Caton was forced to yield up his three titles for destruction at Meynell's hands. Meynell could not sue for another theft: that of his Restoration editor-in-chief, Montague Summers.

From 1927 to 1933 Caton lashed his new-found catch to labour as remorselessly as a galley-master his slave. Summers may have seen advantages even under the heavy load of work Caton piled upon him. Caton's literary tastes were eclectic to say the least, he did not care what work Summers produced so long as he produced it, he paid well, and he shared Summers's enthusiasm for the sort of book antiquarians used to describe as 'curious.' Caton, indeed, was engaged in pirating editions of *Lady Chatterley's Lover* and Norman Douglas's book of limericks and while he had sense enough to have those printed abroad, he sailed with Summers too close to the wind with editions of Sinistrari's *Demoniality,* a treatise on whether succubi and incubi can or cannot 'copulate with human beings' (the verdict comes down heavily on the side of the 'ayes'), and *The Confessions of Madeleine Bavent,* the piece of rabid anti-clericalism against which Summers a few years before in his Kegan Paul publications had been railing. These were seized and a prosecution for obscene libel successfully pursued in 1934.

If Summers found advantages in publishing with Caton he also found disadvantages. Increasing peculiarities in his choice of texts for Fortune, the occasional rather 'gamey' subject-matter, the fact too that Summers was a malicious critic of his fellow-scholars, and suspicions that there had been something worse than carelessness in his recension for Nonesuch of Dryden's dramatic texts, all inveighed against his proper–and it must be said very proper, for he was no mean scholar–estimation as a man of letters. It is only in this light that we can understand why he could only get his pioneering study of the gothic novel, *The Gothic Quest,* published by Caton, a man Summers, mysterious enough himself, dubbed 'the enigma of Belgrave Road.' Yet all through this rather incoherent account of Summers's life–I hear you cry–there seems nothing to link his literary obsessions with his way of life, this curious commixture of spooks and sex and God. Yet a link is there, however vainly Summers attempted to sever it. The link is Anatole James.

The name of course is false, an elision of Anatole France and Henry James, two of his favourite authors. He was the son of a starchy Hull solicitor, born Geoffrey Evans Pickering. Dismissed from his father's house under a cloud–as someone put it, no bigger than a boy's hand–he sought the most obvious advice possible: that of Havelock Ellis. Ellis, then living in Brixton with a mad wife in the attic *à la* Mr Rochester, was uniquely qualified to help. His pioneering book on inversion, although it had suffered the same fate as *Demoniality,* had had wide circulation and, despite his tastes lying elsewhere, had given him a keen insight into the problems of homosexuality. When he heard that Anatole was anxious to make the stage his career he had further resources on which to draw. Ellis had edited several volumes of the old dramatists for the Mermaid series and he knew Montague Summers and his association with The Phoenix. He knew too of Summers's tastes. There could in all directions, he thought, be no more satisfactory introduction. James and Summers met in 1918. They got on instantly. On Boxing Day of that year, to Eton Road, Hampstead, Summers invited James to participate in the Black Mass.

There can be no question of the truth of that. James, although an old man when I knew him, had an exceptional memory; and he was no liar. However, he was an agnostic. I recall his asking me over Sunday breakfast–we were reading the newspapers, that day covering a more than average selection of crimes, wars, disasters, human obliquity in general–if I believed in God. I replied I thought I probably did. 'Very well, then,' Anatole said in his careful, matter-of-fact way, 'if you believe in God, would you not say that, of late, God is being given rather a rough ride?' His agnosticism, rather his utter disbelief in things religious, had rendered the ceremony acutely tedious. He knew enough of such matters to understand he was witnessing a debased form of the Roman Mass, and he had more than a nodding acquaintance with the sexual acts with which it was attended. Other than that he was bored to tears. There were only three people present: Summers, Anatole, and a youth named Sullivan. Anatole was not asked again.

Summers and Anatole continued to meet socially, to carouse in restaurants where Summers arrived made up to the eyes and reeking of scent. Liqueurs were drunk by the pintful, acquaintances of the street afterwards drunkenly sought. Summers confided his especial line of interest. He was aroused only by devout young Catholics, their subsequent corruption giving inexhaustible pleasure. If ever Anatole were able to put such in his direction he would be obliged. Anatole duly did oblige, with an actor named Alfred Farrell. Quite suddenly in 1923 Summers cut Anatole dead in the street. They never spoke again. About that time Summers resigned from the British Society for the Study of Sex Psychology. Three years later, with its fire and its brimstone and its condemnation of witches to the pit of hell, *The History of Witchcraft and Demonology* appeared.

I do not believe as has been suggested that this book and the progressively more outspoken sequels were a pose, their quaint inquisitorial approach employed either to promote sales or to mask Summers's own ungodly activities. My opinion is that from one of his blasphemies, perhaps from their accumulation since 1908, he had learned a terrible lesson. In his shambling, amateur way–and it must be emphasized that he was not the sort of practical, by which I mean intellectual, magician who will guard himself against the dangers inherent in such practices of some sort of psychic kick-back–he had discovered (and not a moment too soon) that the god he worshipped and the god who warred against that god were professionals.

3
R.A.Caton, Montague Summers, and The Fortune Press

I

WHAT connection has Dyian Thomas with a ticket-tout and Wallace Stevens with a pornographer? Who used the printer of *Ulysses* to set up the poems of Lord Alfred Douglas? Why did Cecil Day-Lewis know a slum-landlord in Brighton? Who was Kingsley Amis's first publisher and why did Amis kill him off in one of his novels? Whom did Philip Larkin call a lazy sod?

Reginald Ashley Caton, the common denominator of those questions, would not have been pleased at this investigation of his life and activities. Always elusive, secretive, diffident about imparting any information about his publishing career and totally silent about his private life, he would have felt betrayed by this essay. He was angry enough when, in my bibliography of his most prolific author, Montague Summers, I published evidence that a Roman Catholic book of devotion issued under the imprint of St Peter's Press was the anonymous translation of this equivocal cleric and published by the Fortune Press under a saintly pseudonym. Caton firmly believed that the Vatican had forbidden theological institutions to buy the book solely because of my exposure of translator and publisher despite the *Imprimatur* and *Nihil Obstat* of which both he and Summers were inordinately proud. When I got to know him better he would occasionally throw out a hint here and there but basically he preferred to remain, as Summers once called him in a letter, 'the enigma of Belgrave Road'.

It was not at Belgrave Road but at 12 Buckingham Palace Road in the same area of south-west London that Caton founded the Fortune Press in 1924. He must have adopted his reticence early, for a bookseller who remembered those days told me the press was originally run by 'two Jews'. This was probably because Caton's first imprint was Fortune & Merriman. He used it for only three books, one of them Cecil Day-Lewis's first publication, *Beechen Vigil*; and there never was a Merriman, unless it was Caton's name for an unlikely *alter ego*, and he soon changed the imprint to The Fortune Press. He never tired of saying that fortune never smiled on him. I used to tell him it was because he printed the press's device, a horseshoe, upside down; that is, with the opening in the shoe pointing downwards, a notorious symbol of bad luck. He did not disagree.

He was born on 29 March 1897 at Ashley Gardens, Westminster (hence his second Christian name), the third of four children, two girls and another boy who was killed in the last year of the First World War. The family was always on the move, perhaps giving him the feelings of insecurity he exhibited all his life. They soon left Westminster for 11 and then 22 St Edmund's Terrace, St John's Wood, then Reigate, and finally Roedean Crescent, Brighton, where Caton's father built a house. These moves were precipitated by Caton's mother (née Katy Dyson) who, in contrast to her diligent and hard-working husband, was restless and self-indulgent. Caton was educated at Glengorse preparatory school, Eastbourne, where, to the amusement of the other boys, he arrived for his first day in a sailor suit. There he was taught by my cousin, Ernest Raymond, only a few years older than his pupil, whom he continued to see for a while in London after the war. Ernest recalled Caton ordering lavish dinners in restaurants, insisting on inspecting the cut of meat he had ordered before it was cooked, and smoking large cigars. Perhaps he was hoping to woo a book from the author of the best-selling *Tell England*, for it is hard to imagine Caton indulging in such extravagance to no purpose. From prep school he went on to Rossall and saw a year's war service before joining his father's trade journal for cigar merchants, *Tobacco*, eventually becoming its persuasive and efficient advertisement manager. To his father's annoyance he resigned and began publishing on his own.

He started as he was to end, with modern poetry. However, in 1925 and 1926 the recently founded Nonesuch Press was issuing some elegant limited editions and Caton found himself irresistibly drawn to imitating them. He was young, enthusiastic, determined to make a name for himself but uncritical of and unversed in the laws of copyright. It was probably with no intention to deceive that he issued a slavish imitation of the Nonesuch Press edition of Plato's *Symposium* and copied the typography of two more of their books, Apuleius's *Cupid and Psyche* and the *Kisses* of Johannes Secundus. This was a grave matter and legal proceedings were threatened by both sides, by the

Nonesuch Press for an infringement of copyright and by Caton for its calling the Fortune Press 'thieves and pirates,' but the matter never came to court. Caton withdrew his Plato and delivered up to Nonesuch most of the editions of Apuleius and Secundus for destruction without compensation. However, Caton had not entirely lost the round, discreditable though it was, for he obtained from Nonesuch the services of two of their editors, Shane Leslie, who did further books for him, and Montague Summers, whose collaboration with Caton was to span twenty years.

Caton could never understand why his books were less successful than those of the Nonesuch Press, most of which were spoken for before publication, whereas sheets of some of Caton's more lavish productions languished unbound and unordered for years. After his initial indiscretion he settled into a good house style, Garamond type on either Kelmscott, Arnold, or Batchelor handmade paper, with a stout buckram binding, gilt-lettered and, for the special copies (usually about fifty), vellum boards. But his titles lacked the intrinsic merit of those of his admired rival. They were no more expensive but they hovered around the area which antiquarian booksellers used to describe as 'curious'.

The major reason for his comparative lack of success was his poor distribution. His fierce independence would not permit his employing a regular representative or even a packer. Booksellers, despairing of getting the books they had ordered, gave up trying. He had acute storage problems. When I tried to keep the press going in 1970 and 1971, I often found the required book in one store-room and its dust-jacket in another, two miles away. Caton's love of travel and dislike of the telephone–one bill I settled on his behalf consisted of the rental alone–also campaigned against the very rudiments of publishing efficiency, and much of his time was taken up by the administration of numerous properties in Brighton. He died owning ninety-one houses there, 'not a bathroom among them' he used to boast. He briefly had an arrangement with a local bookseller called Sequana which ended with an obscenity trial in 1934 and also dealt with a chain of 'surgical stores', among whose esoteric artifacts displayed in the windows could often be glimpsed his characteristic yellow dust-wrappers; but he rarely got his books displayed in book shops.

Nevertheless it is hard to understand why, when the Nonesuch editions of the Restoration dramatists edited by Montague Summers went out of print on publication day, Caton's handsomely printed Thomas Shadwell, also edited by Summers, should still have been in print forty-two years after it came out. The five-volume edition cost Caton £2,000, ten times the price of any other of his limited productions and more than ten times his subsequent unlimited novels and poems. He lost some six hundred pounds on the withdrawal of his Nonesuch imitations and by the end of 1927 he was very much out of pocket. There is evidence to suggest he recouped a little of this by a brisk traffic in black-market tickets for Wimbledon and he was not discouraged enough to cease publishing. His subsequent editorial policies aimed at recovering his losses were perhaps regrettable.

He was interested in 'amatory unorthodoxy' and it became a major feature of his list. *The Symposium* was too good a title to abandon altogether; the book was reset twice and sold well. Shane Leslie produced another classical title, a translation of some of the books of the *Greek Anthology* that touch on pederasty, called *Strato's Boyish Muse*. These publications attracted living authors with something to say on such matters and in Caton's list could always be found a fair sprinkling of novels describing the more arcane side of public-school life. One of them was successful enough to be extended into a series called *The Diary of a Boy*, which Caton would sometimes embellish with a printed band announcing it as 'A Book For All Schoolmasters.' So popular did they prove that Caton asked the author to slip a supplementary volume into the annual journal, *Sixteen and a Half*.

His lists also contained a strain of what Auden, writing of A. E. Housman, called 'something to do with violence and the poor': titles such as *Tortures and Torments of the Christian Martyrs, Nell in Bridewell,* a description of the corporal punishments meted out to women in some south German prisons, a novel or two turning on the inevitable consequences of slackness in their duties for young chimney-sweeps and Roman slave-boys, and an original, if discursive study, *Chastisement across the Ages.*

Just before his last illness Caton met me in the Kardomah coffee-house in Piccadilly, around the corner from his basement store-room in Jermyn Street. He entered gaunt, grim-faced, stooping, dressed almost in rags. He was clutching the typescript of a novel recently submitted by a young author, from which he read, in the loud voice he reserved for indiscretions, the opening lines: ' "Yes, I have ——ed a little boy." "Did you burst him in the very depths of his being?"' He was quite surprised when I told him I could not recommend publication. On another occasion, in the same place, he asked me if I were for or against corporal punishment. Again he spoke quite loudly, had not taken his place at the table; was indeed some way off. Without waiting for an answer or noticeably narrowing the distance between us he gave one of his rare chuckles. 'In the old days,' he called out, 'they used a bull's pizzle.'

These swift and alarming departures from reticence were rather a habit of Caton's and he could often come out with some remark that suggested proclivities of a lickerish and recondite order. During Philip Larkin's only meeting with him, for instance, the conversation took a curious turn. They were discussing swear words and their casual use by persons who fail to appreciate their full import when Caton, with an eagerness that made Larkin profoundly uncomfortable, suddenly remarked: 'You hear errand-boys using "sod" for instance. *Do you think they know what it means?*'

Failure to achieve the prestige of the Nonesuch volumes, coupled with enthusiasm for the subjects just mentioned, involved Caton in another, disastrous mistake. On 9 March 1931 he bought 125 shares in a Parisian publishing and bookselling business, Groves & Michaux, and became a director. He then signed an agreement whereby he put 15,000 francs into the firm and became a sleeping partner. Berthe Lessard, Frank Groves's wife, one of the original partners, was to spend all her time running the bookshop, the Librairie du Palais-Royal. Above these handsome premises, which run the whole length of one side of the small Galerie du Palais-Royal, Colette lived for much of her life. Caton could employ this useful retail outlet for some of his publications and at the same time import to London some Groves & Michaux titles. He could also keep abreast of expatriate publishing events in the city and use the storage space in the shop for some of the books he intended to have printed in France.

It is this French connection which has given rise to the rumour that Caton was related to the famous publisher of erotica in Paris, Charles Carrington, and those given to anagrams and word puzzles have pointed out that his surname begins and ends with the same letters as Carrington's. The true connection with Carrington was made by the third partner in the concern, Jean-Albert Michaux. After the war Michaux saw an advertisement in a shop-window in Paris asking for someone to read to a blind man. The man turned out to be Carrington in a sorry state of health and by 1921 Michaux found himself running his shop, 'keeping him going,' as Caton would have put it. Carrington's condition soon took a turn for the worse and, insane as well as blind, he was removed to a *maison de santé* in the south of France. On instructions from his legal trustee, Michaux took over the management of the shop on a formal business basis. After Carrington's death his stock was auctioned at the Hôtel Drouot, and Michaux, with his partner Frank Groves, bought a sizeable portion of it. The residue was on the premises of the Palais-Royal bookshop in December 1930. This we know from the existence of a stock-list probably prepared for Caton. It makes fascinating reading. Most French authors were kept at the shop and there were also standard English writers, reference books, and atlases. Caton supplied several of his Fortune publications: Shadwell, of course; Charlotte Dacre's *Zofloya*; John Downes's *Roscius Anglicanus*; Summers's *Essays in Petto* and Lord Alfred Douglas's *Satires*; Beresford Egan and 'Brian de Shane's' pictorial satire, *De Sade*. As well as the good old stand-bys of 'gallant' literature, Paul de Kock, Strapa-rola, the yellow-wrapped 'Bibliothèque des Curieux' series published by their fellow-publishers the Briffaut brothers, Groves & Michaux's stock boasted a darker *enfer* derived from Carrington: *The Old Man Young Again, The Plague of Lust, The Town Bull in the Elysian Fields, Mysteries of Verbena House,* and two titles Caton was to reprint in London, Brantôme's *Lives of Fair and Gallant Ladies* and the Byronic pastiche, *Don Leon.* Also in the inventory are the original woodblocks for the illustrated edition of *The Picture of Dorian Gray* issued by Carrington in 1910 and the manuscript of a translation of Huysmans's *Là-bas* by Alfred Allinson. Allinson is an elusive literary figure who did quite a lot of translating for Carrington sometimes under his own name and sometimes, for racier titles, as 'an Oxford M.A.' Groves & Michaux published the *Là-bas* translation and Caton purchased some sheets which he issued in London with his own Fortune Press imprint.

Certain documents found after Caton's death in a Paris safe-deposit indicate that at this time he was also wholesaling unauthorized editions of Norman Douglas's *Some Limericks* and of Lawrence's *Lady Chatterley.* Their respective bibliographers record pirated continental editions appearing on the market in 1930 but do not lay the responsibility at any door. Caton, if not himself the perpetrator, at least had access to the source of the piracies, printed apparently at Leipzig by Oscar Brandstetter, Dresdner-Strasse 11-13. Apart from this he did not achieve very much in Paris and later claimed that he had been cheated by the Groves and by an American called Leonard. He chose Maurice Darantière, the long-suffering printer of *Ulysses,* to do some books for him: John Cleland's *Memoirs of a Coxcomb* and Douglas's *Collected Satires,* an elegant small folio which Douglas said reflected much credit on Caton.

He sold his shares in the Palais-Royal bookshop to a Mme Bouquin in February 1932 but three years later, presumably after Frank Groves's departure, reopened negotiations with Mme Lessard and a new partner, Mme Legarde. Some of his titles were again displayed in the shop and for two novels, a translation from the Hungarian and a story of preparatory school life by 'Esmond Quinterley' (the author of the best-selling 'Boy' diaries), he used the imprint 'Paris, Palais-Royal Beaujolais Library.'

In 1934 Caton was struck another blow. He was prosecuted for obscene libel. It all started with a police raid near Caton's office, on the Sequana bookshop, where some of his books were stocked. They were seized and publisher and bookseller arraigned 'to show cause why a number of books, papers, writings, prints, pictures and drawings, alleged to be obscene and kept on the premises for the purpose of gain, should not be destroyed.' It is interesting to note that for the defence of one of them, *The Confessions of Madeleine Bavent,* Caton's solicitor hoped to call the eminent anthropologist Bronislaw Malinowski, but he was unable to appear at the last moment and, despite alternative evidence, the magistrate ordered the book's destruction.

II

At eleven o'clock in the morning of 25 February 1927, at 12 Buckingham Palace Road, Caton first met Montague Summers. Summers, then forty-six, had been educated at Clifton College and Trinity, Oxford and, after an indiscreet volume of verse, *Antinous and Other Poems* (how well it would have looked in Caton's list) he settled down to his study of witchcraft, the drama of the Restoration, and the Gothic novel.

His inquisitorial denunciation of black magic in his several books, couched for the most part–as he himself admitted–in the style of John Addington Symonds and in forgotten canting phrases of the late seventeenth century, has been viewed with suspicion, since there is evidence that as a young man he was no stranger to such practices himself, but it seems that his condemnation was sincere, the result perhaps of some psychic shock he had received. Some of the scholarship displayed in his editions of Restoration dramatists has also been called into question, but there can be no doubt that if it had not been for his enthusiasm and panache in his resuscitation of the English playwrights from 1660 to 1710, not only in print but on the boards, we should not be seeing today (although we do not see nearly enough) any of this enormously rich vein of our theatrical heritage.

We can presume it was Caton's interest in the Nonesuch Press that led him to Summers, Summers having edited its editions of Congreve, Wycherley, and Otway–the last published only four days before their first meeting. Summers was still under contract to edit the plays of Dryden but he and Caton laid plans that day to publish editions of John Oldham and Rochester and to bring along for Caton's inspection 'the French edition of those Latin poems of which I spoke.' This might have been the Liseux (1885) edition of the *Elegies of Pacifico Massimi* of which Caton printed but never published a selection or a French translation of Strato which Shane Leslie put into English.

Summers also agreed to undertake a translation of Juvenal–like the other projects to be kept a secret. The day after they met Summers was offering yet more: 'There are two Restoration dramatists calling loudly for an editor–Shadwell and Southerne.' This is the first reference to the project which was to result in Caton's most expensive venture, published as soon as 8 December of the same year.

A contract was drawn up retaining Summers's services and he promised to sign with no other publisher without first consulting Caton. In March plans for Oldham and Rochester had been shelved, probably because of John Hayward's edition of the latter which Summers was to tear to shreds in his

Playhouse of Pepys. Work began on Shadwell, however, and Summers drew his publisher's attention to *Demoniality*, destined to suffer destruction at the hands of the police. By the second week of April, Summers delivered the manuscript of his Introduction for this and got his fee of £35, leaving him free, as he hoped, to work on Shadwell. Finished copies of *Demoniality* reached Summers on 6 June and he thought it 'an admirable production'. This letter of acknowledgment and appreciation is the first to begin 'Dear Mr Gaton' instead of 'Dear Sir'. The slip was never corrected.

By now another project was under discussion: an English translation of Thomas Sanchez of Cordova's *De Matrimonio* (1602), 'truly a very storehouse of curious facts,' says Summers, who was fascinated by the book and claimed to have introduced its secrets to George Moore and Sir Edmund Gosse. The planned publication was abandoned as it was considered to be too long. The Whitefriars Press was beginning to set the Shadwell text with Summers still busy at the notes. Caton was pressing hard. He wanted an announcement of their Southerne to be included in the current Fortune Press prospectus and he had also persuaded Summers to embark on an edition of a seventeenth century anthology of theatrical verses, *Covent Garden Drollery.* On 12 July 1927, Summers writes:

> In order to get the work thro' I have had to engage an expert typist temporarily–which is rather an expensive job. I am running CGD along with the Shadwell, and will let you have it in a fortnight's time. In order to get the work done I have had to break a contract with another house, which is rather tiresome–So I am sure you will not mind if I ask you to advance me £30 on my *Shadwell* and *C-G-D* fees.

In the same letter he agrees to edit yet another book, John Downes's *Roscius Anglicanus* but points out that the critical apparatus will be a long job. This was true, for sixty-odd pages of text eventually required more than 200 of explanatory notes.

Throughout the summer, Caton's editor worked and worked on Shadwell and only on 23 November did he get the final proofs off to the printer, but before that, in late August, hard pressed and still employing a costly typist, he was beginning to think about the book's reception. He asked Caton not to let *The Times Literary Supplement* have advance news of its existence, perhaps because of John Hayward's connections there, and sternly warned against sending a review copy to *The Nation and Athenaeum*: 'One or two men do the reviewing who never miss an opportunity of referring to my work in a most disparaging way–It is largely personal, since I have for my part candidly said what I think of the lucubrations of the gentlemen...' At the same time he informs Caton he is constantly asked for copies of his essay on the Marquis de Sade, originally published in pamphlet form 'for adult students of Social

Questions,' and suggests printing it with a few other of his essays. This is the first reference to what became *Essays in Petto.*

The Nonesuch Press was now beginning to lean on Summers for his copy for their Dryden, which he had been under contract to produce for a long time. Summers had just signed with Caton for an edition of Southerne. Which was to come first?

Covent Garden Drollery was still not out and Caton got wind of the Dobell edition to be edited by G.Thorn-Drury, a scholar with whom Summers was on excellent terms, and urged Summers to make all speed with his own editorial matter. Summers complied, but warned Caton he could not attempt anything of the kind again 'as it has very nearly knocked me up, and that will never do with Shadwell to be finished.' The book appeared in October 1927 and on 8 December the five-volume Shadwell was published to some acclaim. In January 1928 *Petto* was ready for the printer. Summers had thought of reproducing as a frontispiece a caricature of himself which had appeared in the *Evening Standard* a few years earlier. It depicts Summers in clerical collar, spats, and polished black shoes, balancing a teacup on his knee and waxing lyrical over some literary point. Caton may have thought it a little frivolous, for a portrait photograph was preferred and Summers duly went to Vaughan & Freeman for a studio sitting. The results did not please everyone to whom he showed them and he had another sitting with a new firm, 'in several positions.' It is in this letter, describing the second session, that he begins to hint at delays and difficulties: 'I hear that shortly the Nonesuch people will be pressing me for the Dryden,' he writes and adds that although *Roscius* is getting on well he would be grateful for the fee. Five days later Caton sent him £35 but in his acknowledgment Summers advised there could now be no doubt the Nonesuch Press was 'aggrieved'.

Marking his letter 'Personal', which must mean that Summers still did not know that Caton worked alone, he wrote on 27 April to say he suspected '[Francis] Birrell and [David] Garnett' reviewed his books for *The Times Literary Supplement* and that this explained the hostile criticisms. Birrell and Garnett knew Francis Meynell, founder of Nonesuch, and his wife Vera who shared their dislike of Summers. If they hated him while he was in their employ they were even more incensed at his departure. Summers writes to Caton in another 'Personal' letter of 31 May: 'This lack of recognition is becoming rather serious from my point of view. There can be no doubt that the break with the Nonesuch Press, although it was not of my seeking, has done me a great deal of harm in various quarters, for they must have far more influence than one supposed.'

From Caton's point of view, nothing had been settled about the future. Was Summers to edit (anonymously) an edition of Aristophanes, to do the little Rochester despite its bulky Bloomsbury rival, to produce a collection of early witchcraft tracts? And which was to be done first?

At last, in November 1928, *Roscius* appeared. Summers was pleased with the production, as he invariably was with Caton's books, but was sorry not to see his name on the spine of the jacket. Relations were still cordial at the end of the year and in the early part of 1929 Caton took the trouble to procure for Summers a copy of *The Well of Loneliness*. By March, Summers had still not paid for it and in explanation wrote that the death of a sister and brother had kept him from his desk. He remained elusive throughout the spring and summer but in a rare communication on 15 July opined that he did not think that the delays mattered: 'rather the contrary. It has been pointed out to me that in 1927-8 my output was really too large...Brett Smith was 10 years on his Etherege, 2 small vols.; and Pinto was working for 5 years on his Sedley...So I must not be pressed or I shall not do myself justice.' There is clearly some truth in Summers's reference to his over-exposure, for in the two years in question he had published four original works and edited ten others. On 24 September, 'having been moving about the country,' he wrote: 'I am bound to confess I have the gravest doubts of publishing a Rochester.' It was time for Caton to strike. He wrote to Summers on 1 October 1929 threatening legal action for breaches of contract. He did not hear until 4 November, when Summers wrote:

> In 1927 I did eight books for the Fortune Press...in 1928 I did two...I think you hardly appreciate what a terrific output this is. Most writers would have required two or three years for the Shadwell alone. I was working at immense pressure which is quite impossible to sustain. I am as anxious as yourself that the two books, the Bavent and the other volume should be completed.
>
> As you are aware I put aside much work for other publishers in order to give the Fortune Press the precedence.
>
> I have contracts waiting for other publishers made in 1926 & earlier, and it is only fair that after having supplied the Fortune Press with so much material I should now satisfy some of these long outstanding claims...
>
> I must ask you not to importune me so urgently. It is most distracting, and I will add most unusual.
>
> I have never before been thus pressed by any publisher, and you oblige me to point out that the agreement for these two books does not specify any date of delivery of copy...
>
> Please accept my reasonable assurance that the work will be done as soon as possible...

Still no copy arrived and Caton wrote another stiff letter on 15 March

1930. The summer of that year passed and nothing came from his editor's pen. There can be no doubt that Summers was closeted with the arduous Dryden work and had not a moment for Caton's projects. At this point the correspondence breaks off. Caton consulted his lawyers and a writ was issued. Caton claimed that by Summers's breaches of the Rochester and Bavent contracts and advanced fees he had lost £946 in outlays and profits.

After the case was over (the result is not known and it may have been settled out of court) defendant and plaintiff continued their collaboration but it had inevitably grown uneasy. After the mammoth volume *The Gothic Quest* and its supplement *A Gothic Bibliography* had appeared, relations between them appear finally to cease; few letters survive the war and post-war period. In 1946 Summers provided some rather sketchy notes for Caton's latest edition of *Là-Bas,* but this was the final work he did for him.

III

Caton was now very much involved in his poetry list and had for some time been slowly abandoning his policy of publishing only de luxe editions. The decision may have been taken because of the obscenity trial which had shaken him badly and which he never forgot. Twelve years afterwards he accepted Philip Larkin's novel *Jill,* but the printer refused to set parts of it as they contained four-letter words. In the tea-shop where they met to discuss the matter, Caton remarked that to find yourself in the dock on an obscenity charge was 'no joke.' He used to tell me for months after the trial he was followed by plain-clothes men. Perhaps he was.

He had published a little poetry at the very beginning–T. W. H. Crosland, Cecil Day-Lewis, and Lord Alfred Douglas–so the idea was not entirely new, but these had been done in limited editions and had not reflected a particularly new wave of writing. Because of earlier hoarding of paper, he was the only publisher during the Second World War with sufficient stocks to be able to risk very much in the way of new work, and the list he built up from 1939 to the early 1960's is vastly impressive. Appearing either in anthologies or in separate collections are John Wain, Elizabeth Jennings, Kingsley Amis, Charles Causley, Gavin Ewart, 'John Gawsworth,' Lawrence Durrell, Ruthven Todd, Rayner Heppenstall, Francis King, Cecil Roberts, Thom Gunn, Wrey Gardiner, Paul Goodman, Ted Hughes, Tambimuttu, Philip Larkin, Sylvia Plath, Wallace Stevens, and Dylan Thomas.

To produce his poetry books, he employed printers all over England. Dissatisfied with the efforts of the current one or to ferret out a cheaper successor, he travelled to visit printing works at Poole, Bristol, Haywards Heath, Whitstable, Woodchester, Redhill, Faversham, Hove, Worcester, Tonbridge, Lewes, Erith, Ashford, Ramsgate, Chichester, Compton Chamberlayne, Tunbridge Wells, and Canterbury. It must be remembered, too, that he had to spend considerable time managing his ninety-one house properties in Brighton, and to attend to literary and commercial matters he was forced to make the train journey between London and Brighton several times a day, scouring the carriages for discarded newspapers.

On one of these many journeys an unfortunate incident occurred. His thoughts elsewhere or harried by the imminent departure of the train, Caton got in to the guard's van by mistake, and found himself unable to get into the corridor. Stout wire netting barred his way. The reason for this was to prevent from straying into passenger accommodation the only other occupant of the van, a large goat. Unluckily, a writer contemplating sending his manuscript to Fortune, but advised of its proprietor's eccentricities, passed along the corridor and came across the incarcerated couple, juxtaposition of the animal and his prospective publisher giving considerable alarm.

Caton often remarked that there was no money in poetry but his authors sometimes thought differently and there could be rows about what was owing. A story has it that Caton was threatened by one of his poets with a loaded pistol. Others were made to buy considerable numbers of copies of their books or to become their own, unpaid, representatives and most, Kingsley Amis and Philip Larkin included, never received a penny piece for their work.

One writer on Caton's list who, behind his back, nicknamed him Satan, was visited unexpectedly–Caton was always keen to inspect his author's houses–in his remote country cottage. Caton thundered on the door–another habit. On being admitted he mentioned he had travelled a considerable distance by omnibus and required refreshment. Would Mr Caton stay for lunch? That depended on what there was to eat. The poet said he would ask his wife. Caton appeared startled, snapped out: 'What?' then fell silent and seemed hurt. 'It's a pity you're married,' he said at last. 'Husbands don't make such good poets.' Luncheon turned out to be roast beef and Caton agreed to stay. Time wore on and not until tea-time did he show signs of leaving. 'I hope you'll drive me to my bus-stop,' he said as he got to his feet, 'and perhaps...get your wife to prepare some sandwiches for my journey–cheese ones.' Again the poet's wife was consulted on what might be available. There was only cheddar. 'H'm,' said Caton, 'no Danish blue?'

Not all poets were so badly treated. Some had to pay for publication, of course, or, as Caton put it, 'help me out'; but at least one author received an unsolicited cash payment and an offer to publish unseen whatever poems he might care to send.

Caton published Kingsley Amis's first book, *Bright November*. Scurvily treated by him, Amis put Caton into five of his novels, changing his initials to ' L.S.' and eventually killing him off in *The Anti-Death League*. He figures largest in *Lucky Jim,* where he is found editing an academic journal to which Jim Dixon submits an article on 'The Economic Influence of the Development in Shipbuilding Technique, 1450 to 1485.' L.S. prevaricates about publication and eventually Dixon discovers that he has been appointed to the Chair of History of Commerce, University of Tucumán, Argentina, and has stolen the article for publication under his own name in a luxurious Italian periodical. (Amis was actually asked by the University of Tucumán to write a short book on Graham Greene which it neither published nor paid for so it seemed a suitable place for L.S.Caton to find employment.)

Again, the librarian-hero of *That Uncertain Feeling* is handed a piece of paper by a colleague: 'a sheet hastily torn from a pad bearing a few ill-written lines in green ink. Without formality the writer announced that he was thinking of emigrating to the Argentine, would like the recipient of his note to look out some books about that region and would call in to fetch them "in due course". He'd be writing again "before very long" and signed himself "L. S. Caton". I crumpled all this up and threw it down the main steps into the street.' In *Take a Girl Like You,* some schoolmasters examine a letter: 'without formality the writer announced that he had finally returned from an academic appointment in the Argentine, had been preparing a talk on the educational institutions of that region, and would be available for its delivery "in due course". He would be writing again "before very long" and signed himself "L. S. Caton".' And he appears again in *One Fat Englishman*: 'without formality the writer announced that he had recently arrived in the United States from the United Kingdom, wanted assistance in finding a publisher for a book of his about South America, considered chiefly from educational and other social points of view, and would be sending the typescript along "in due course". He would be writing again "before very long" and signed himself "L. S. Caton".' In *The Anti-Death League*, poised to give his lecture, Caton is shot to pieces, his remains barely identifiable. 'L.S.' stands for 'Lazy Sod.' At the time they fell into Caton's clutches, Amis and Philip Larkin were amusing themselves by inventing imaginary jazz groups and records based on literary personalities. Lazy Sod Caton was analogous to Sleepy John Estes or Blind Boy Fuller, both well-known blues singers. Larkin recalls that they had Caton recording 'I Ain't Lazy, I'm Just Dreamin'.'

Another novelist to put Caton in a book is George Sims, author of two works published by Fortune, who depicts him in his first novel, *The Terrible Door,* as the seedy, prune-eating Charlie Hayter, proprietor of the Bon-Ton Literary and Publicity Agency.

By the end of the 1950s Caton was debating selling his business, but could not make up his mind to part with it or to decide on a price; not that he needed the money—'I don't have to do this,' he would often remark to authors pressing for action—but because he thought the prestige of his press demanded a sizeable offer and he delayed for too long doing anything practical about a sale. His health was now declining and he underwent a serious operation for cancer of the throat. Although he made a complete recovery he found the press more and more difficult to run. His sister, disturbed at the state of his health and reclusive ways, repeatedly asked him to come and share her house in Rottingdean, but he refused. She did not even know where he was living. Eventually she was forced to follow him secretly from the railway station to a house in Brighton where he had a room on the top floor.

He lived mainly out of tins, although he was sometimes glimpsed, late on a Saturday afternoon, struggling through the streets with a carcass of meat bought cheaply from a butcher about to shut up shop for the weekend. He habitually wore fearfully old and grubby clothes, an RAF sergeant's raincoat—the stitching which had held the stripes still visible on the arms—sports shirts with frayed ties holding together the buttonless collars, stained cotton trousers, two pairs at once in cold weather, neither correctly buttoned. He would apologize for his appearance, explaining that he dressed as he did because he did not want his tenants, regularly visited for outstanding rent, to know he had any money to carry out the numerous repairs his houses needed. When we should dine at the Mirabelle, a plan often mooted but never realized because of a mutual vagueness about who would foot the bill, he assured me he would dress up.

He had ignored my letters requesting information for my bibliography of Montague Summers and I am sure that it was as a possible purchaser of the press and not to make up for past inattention that in 1968 he eventually approached me.

I was managing the rare book department of The Times Bookshop. He called in the afternoon suggesting Debenham and Freebody's as a suitable place for tea and a chat. I explained that the bookshop was being closed down and that a friend and I were going to open a small antiquarian book-business in Gloucester Place.

We agreed to publish a retrospective catalogue of such of his publications as were still in print, and this, listing 182 titles, duly appeared in 1969.

Caton, though continuing to urge me to buy the whole business or at least to issue a larger, more comprehensive catalogue, which he wanted printed at the Curwen Press, was happy to supply books that our customers ordered, but during this period I never set foot in either of his store-rooms or in his office in Belgrave Road, where he had moved at the end of the war. I had to write to him with my requirements which he would unearth and then deliver at the Kardomah coffee-house in Piccadilly, a favoured rendezvous since he liked to watch the mechanical footmen on Fortnum's clock appear on the hour. If the books ordered were too many to carry, he would come by taxi and bang persistently on our front door until I opened it.

In June 1970 he collapsed on the Brighton train and was taken to Westminster Hospital. His sister sent me the first of many letters written at his dictation to tell me the news. From his sick-bed he pointed out the necessity of my 'keeping him going' in his absence. I agreed to do so, partly because it would give me access to his premises to get the books I needed to fill orders. There was a long silence when I asked for the keys. He was wrestling with the distasteful realization that someone else would penetrate his secret rooms. Some authors, none speaking highly of tidiness or salubrity, had visited Belgrave Road, but I was probably the only person who went to his other two London stores. Eventually he handed over the keys.

The routine of 'keeping him going' was soon learnt. First the letters had to be collected from the post-office at Howick Place where he had had a box for many years. From there they were taken to Belgrave Road, the head office, as it were. Entrance was made down the area steps and through a double-locked front door giving on to a damp front entrance-hall stacked high with old newspapers, packets of unbound sheets of books considered even by Caton to be unsaleable, and string. Another locked door gave access to the office itself. Parcels were piled to the ceiling, long flat ones of dust-jackets, thick heavy ones of bound books, packing-cases of sewn sheets, not only around the walls but almost solidly through the whole area of the room. The floor, the only really suitable place for loose papers, had been used for this purpose over the years so that a rich uneven wadding had formed over the concrete floor, firm and damp in some places, flimsy and brittle in others. Under a long working-bench on one side of the room Caton had regularly cast empty milk bottles, most of them unwashed, until they were packed solid. There was a desk facing the grimy barred window which gave on to the area, but its folding top and multitudinous pigeon-holes held such a mass of loose papers, documents bundled into old envelopes, keys, bottles of patent medicines, half-empty packets of cigars and cigarettes, that it seemed an extension of the general muddle and decay.

Then one proceeded to a hot, dusty, store-room with an adjoining cubby-hole next to the boiler-house in the basement of Terminal House, Grosvenor Gardens. There had been trouble over the rent there, nominal though it must have been. Finally one went to 58 Jermyn Street, another basement, a long dark room with books in several bays. There was a large collection of threepenny bits and quite a few rusted tins of anchovy paste. The floor was carpeted with sheets from an outdated, but once comprehensive mail-order catalogue of children's underclothing.

These were difficult times, for Caton on his sick-bed and later at his sister's, where she eventually persuaded him to go, was very demanding. At the time of his stroke he was disputing an advertising account to no avail, and at last bailiffs broke into Belgrave Road and took away his old and treasured typewriter, the only object of value they could find. The landlord was urging me to have the basement cleared, fearing there was a risk of fire, so grudging permission was given for the rubbish to be removed. Supervision of this operation was imperative, Caton said, since small caches of food, clothes, tobacco, would come to light and careful sifting would be necessary before anything at all was carried away.

These finds, and other objects from the other two rooms, had to be ferried to Rottingdean at regular intervals and as well as things from the office I often had to take a pound of sweetish, dark-brown Scandinavian cheese, more like fudge in taste and texture, of which Caton was inordinately fond, sometimes falling on it the minute I arrived. He sat in the best chair in the drawing-room, the best room in the house, surrounded by newspapers which he would read one spread at a time and then allow to fall to the floor until he was almost buried in newsprint. His sister left us alone to talk business but on one occasion came in to tidy the cushions. He looked at her suspiciously: 'You're not going to sit down, are you?' he asked. Another time over lunch he suddenly swooped on my plate with his knife and fork, whisking away to his own one of my two lamb cutlets. His sister remonstrated with him loudly but he merely claimed I could not possibly manage two, and tucked in.

He was now resigned to selling the press for a tithe of the figure he originally had in mind, but what came to everybody except the purchaser as a relief weighed him down still further. He could not contemplate life without his publishing. He slowly grew weaker, began to refuse food, suspecting that it was poisoned. On 17 July 1971, he died. He left £129,251 to the Preservation Society and St Margaret's Church, Rottingdean. Grim, unlovable, he had published more than 600 books.

4
Ralph Nicholas Chubb: Prophet and Paederast

RALPH NICHOLAS CHUBB was born at Harpenden, Hertfordshire, on 8 February 1892. Four months after his birth, his family moved to the cathedral town of St Albans, where he was educated at the grammar school built beneath the walls of the Abbey, a building which came to symbolize for him a deeply significant experience and in the gatehouse of which his oil-painting, *The Furnace of Creation*, once hung. He won a scholarship to Selwyn College, Cambridge, in 1910, and, gathering himself a Blue for chess–a game learned in childhood and enjoyed not only for its skill but for its evocation of childhood memories–he proceeded BA in 1913. On 27 November 1914, he enlisted in the army, attained the rank of Captain, was mentioned in despatches at Loos in September 1915, but was invalided out with severe neurasthenia before the war ended. For a short time afterwards he lived in London, studying at the Slade School of Art. Throughout the twenties he exhibited his oils and watercolours at many of the leading London galleries. His oil, *Ganymede*, was exhibited at the Royal Academy in 1925.

He left London in 1921 to move with his sister, Muriel, and brother, Lawrence, to Curridge, Berkshire. There the two brothers built from an old carpenter's bench and some odd pieces of timber a crude printing-press on which Lawrence printed his *Vision* in 1924 in an edition of twenty-seven copies and on which Ralph printed his first three books, *Manhood* (1924), *The Sacrifice of Youth* (1925), and *A Fable of Love and War* (1925). He abandoned the press when he and his sister moved to Fair Oak Cottage, Ashford Hill, on the borders of Berkshire and Hampshire in 1927, where he was to remain for the rest of his life. It is ironic that at Aldermaston, a few miles from the tiled cottage where the war-scarred, peace-loving poet lived, the huge atomic weapons research establishment was erected in the last year of his life.

Between 1927 and 1930 Chubb possessed no printing-press and had his poems commercially produced, but during this period he was contemplating the production of a perfect book. 'I always visualized,' he wrote, 'a method which would combine poetical idea, script, and designs, in free and harmonious rhythm–all unified together–so as to be mutually dependent and significant.'[1]

In 1929, he produced a short book, *An Appendix,* on a duplicating machine which, with its ability to reproduce drawings and manuscript without the aid of metal types and blocks, was the preliminary step to his acquiring a lithographic press. The next year he finished a calligraphic manuscript, *The Book of Visions of Nature and Supernature, Solar and Lunar,* the format of which heralds the work that was to follow. In June 1931, his dream was realized and his first lithographic book, *The Sun Spirit: a Visionary Phantasy,* was finished. Like the three that succeed it, it is a tall folio; no metal types are used and the whole is a lithographic reproduction of the author's original holograph and illustrations. It is not really possible to give an accurate idea of the complexity–one is tempted to say, tangle–of the eight books which Chubb produced in this medium. It took him three years to print *The Heavenly Cupid, Water-Cherubs* and *The Child of Dawn,* two to print *The Secret Country,* and six to complete *Flames of Sunrise.* He pulled sheaves of proofs on cheap stock until inking and pressure were exactly as he wanted, noting the faults in the margins of the sheets for future correction. For the final printing–and often for the later, trial proofs also–he used only the finest handmade paper. A handful of copies of the already drastically limited editions he embellished by illuminating certain pages in watercolour and in gold.

For thirty years Chubb toiled at these books in the little wooden studio he built in the copse ('Benskin's Copse' of *The Secret Country* imprint), leaving home for occasional trips to London to hawk his huge volumes round the bookshops, his own delivery man as well as his own printer, publisher, and publicity agent. He had completed the text of what was to have been his last book, *The Golden City,* at his death on 14 January 1960. His sister called in an expert from the neighbouring University of Reading to complete the lithographing; the finished sheets were transferred to London for binding and returned to Fair Oak Cottage for her to distribute. The task was not heavy, for the entire edition numbered only eighteen copies.

Chubb's books show a development of technique–from the handmade press fashioned from the screw of a carpenter's bench and odd bits of wood to a highly efficient lithographic process such as no private press owner has yet attempted to imitate[2]–but this technical expertise is in direct contradiction to his literary talent. As practical ability increases so does the pathological breakup of thought, expression, and intent. The rugged simplicity of the early verse, 'prentice work truly, but excusable as authors' juvenilia are, swells turgidly into the high-flown prophetic cant of the bulk of the lithographed books and finally descends woefully, in *Treasure Trove* and *The Golden City*, into uninspired tales of fairies, elves, knights, dragons, maidens in distress, all the trappings of an outdated and untalented nursery. In appearance the works fall into three distinct groups, this outward format corresponding to the changing themes expressed within the covers. Thus we find the early poems with the rough woodcuts and coarse paper; the four pre-war lithographic folios; and the four post-war lithographic quartos, the three groups looking dissimilar at the most casual of glances and upholding the dissimilarity in their contents. From an early interest in manhood and boyhood, Chubb moves to proclamations of a form of spiritual 'democracy' not unlike the creeds of Walt Whitman and Edward Carpenter, and calls for a return to nature in accordance with the dynamic, divine spark within every human. As one reads Chubb chronologically one is aware of an ever-increasing obsession with paederasty, hinted at from the very start but with each new publication becoming ever more intrusive. This trait eventually comes to occupy the central core of his work and Chubb expounds in detail an occult, mystical philosophy which he hopes will transcend the physical love of boys and raise it to the realms of a religious experience, Such a fantastic, unpractical devotion proves to Chubb impossible to found and, no converts having been discovered, he reverts to childhood tales of buttercup-haired pages and insipid adaptations of the legends of King Arthur, a catastrophic, disillusioned flight to the security of early childhood memories and the only substitute, albeit a pathetic one, for the ideal creed which Chubb had early envisaged and of which he had once been absolutely, because divinely, assured.

The events in Chubb's life which gave him the impetus to write and to try to retain or regain his adolescence through a form of spiritual alchemy were five in number: the sight he experienced at an early age of some village boys bathing naked; the discovery of masturbation; a passionate attachment to an unknown choir-boy; a love-affair when he was eighteen with a boy three years his junior; and his witnessing the death of a young soldier in battle.

Some of these traumas are spoken of in the first of his lithographic books, *The Sun Spirit* (1931), a chimerical fantasy in which an aged seer (Chubb's wiser self) takes a youthful disciple through a series of visions, culminating in the visible appearance of Satan whom the youth must overcome before he may achieve perfect harmony of soul. In one of the scenes, a grizzled phantom, symbolic of Chubb's lower nature, rises from a pit of flames, which the disciple must face unafraid as a prerequisite of his spiritual rebirth. The phantom recalls Chubb's childhood; through his words the disciple is told that Chubb suffered from uncontrollable nightly terrors and, at puberty, from an obsession that he harboured a secret vice, at the same time labouring under a physical deformity ignored by his friends only through their tact. Of the former fear, no reader needs telling that the secret vice is masturbation; indeed Chubb continues by describing his first act of self-abuse. He straddles his rocking-horse and begins to rock: 'I squeezed harder and harder upon the cushion-pad. My face flushed my eyes sparkled. My heart beat faster faster. Thrills passed through me. I had a moment of ecstasy. Suddenly a chill of disgust came over me.' He slunk into bed just before his father entered the room to divine from his guilty face the cause of his embarrassment. Thenceforward Chubb was unable to face his schoolfellows for he believed his features betrayed his secret, but nightly and alone his addiction to the self-induced sexual pleasure was gratified. To enhance the excitement he employed the vivid memory of a scene he had witnessed when he was eight years old and had always harboured, of a group of village boys romping stark naked by the seashore. 'Their forms were white and smooth like lilies. My young heart ached with longing.' Masturbating, he would imagine their 'invisible bodies...towselling in unlicensed intercourse.'

At the age of eighteen, the other three events occurred. In the Abbey of St Albans he saw a choir-boy. 'Instantly our souls flew to meet each other in wild embrace,' he says in *The Sun Spirit*; 'Such was the awakening of my spring. My eyes were open'd to love.' He enlarges on the incident in *Flames of Sunrise* (1954) where he tells us that he and the boy never met but that he longed passionately 'to be his boy-bride.' Sunday after Sunday he gazed at the boy until, one day when he thought himself alone in the Abbey and was standing to listen to a Bach fugue being performed on the organ, he caught sight of the boy standing there also. He made up his mind to speak to him but the boy hastily left the building and, joining a group of his friends outside, walked out of Chubb's life.

In the same year, Chubb was luckier in meeting a boy of fifteen with whom he had his first and last pleasurable sexual relationship:

Idling we pass'd our sunny days bathing in sequester'd streams, Sprawling with gold-brown bodies side-by-side beneath the noonday beam, Fondling, spending, silently embracing. The mounting heat, the shorten'd breath, the surging onslaught of desire, Sweet pulsing short-lived agony seeking relief, the brimming consummation and flood, The drooping languor, the heavenly listless content with bright swimming pupils gazing up seraphical at the azure vault. (*The Sun Spirit*)

Then came the war. Chubb volunteered and in the fighting watched the slaughter of a boy, a creature such as those he had always mentally, and once physically, loved. He was the curly-haired, seventeen-year old son of a blacksmith and is referred to in the poetical sequence 'Midway through Life', in *The Heavenly Cupid* (1934). His death symbolized for Chubb all the horrors and the taboos of society. The boy, a beloved object, was not only forbidden by law to be loved by an adult male but was legally sacrificed by the same laws in the service of his country. In Chubb's neurasthenic condition, the images of boyhood impinged on his mind at that moment of bloodshed: the sight and touch of beautiful lads ending with their frightful death in a wanton slaughter. The snatching of the blacksmith's boy from his side displayed, in one action, mankind's refusal to accept a boy's beauty and its readiness to have him murdered for its own ends. The spark of Chubb's prophetic fire had been struck. He would be the redeemer of English boyhood, the prophet thundering its call for love and freedom into ears long deafened by wars and bourgeois customs. For the lads of Britain he would speak:

> My staunch young brothers, I know you! Your bard has arisen at last! When you sweat at the mills I am with you. When the siren hoots, And off you run with your towels and strip to the skin and plunge From the black lock-gate in the pool and wash off the grime and the sweat.[3]

It is in his second book, *The Sacrifice of Youth*, that Chubb first exercises his ideas of the slaughter of the boy by society, adding also an echo of his childish nightmare terrors in the depiction of a raging beast to whom an unnamed tribe must ritually sacrifice a beautiful nude youngster. In the same year, 1922, he wrote a longer poem, 'The Ballad of the Forest,' which remains unpublished apart from twenty-two lines which appear in *Songs of Mankind*(1930). This poem incorporates a shorter one, in a different metre from the body of the work, the content of which indicates that another of Chubb's obsessions was already at work. In this short interpolated poem is described a visit he made to a bathing-place where boys and maidens (the latter were soon to be dropped from Chubb's fantasies except for being vehicles for the birth and nurture of the boy-child) strip naked to swim unmolested until one day they are discovered by two horrified adults and driven from the water. This failure by mankind to accept adolescent physical beauty is a variation on the condoning of adolescent slaughter and it is clear from *The Sacrifice of Youth* and 'The Ballad of the Forest' that these two problems were in Chubb's mind before he began the composition of the later prophetic lithographed folios. Soon the banished boys were to become angels and their little wooded bathing-places sacrosanct areas of ritual baptism.

Also in February 1922 Chubb compiled *A Fable of Love and War,* the first of his writings overtly to suggest his sympathy with physical intimacies between man and boy, while continuing to present his images of war and murder. A boy meets a mighty warrior in a forest, declares his love for him, and attempts, unsuccessfully, to seduce him using the cunning argument that 'Pollen's not *all* for fruitful cells: / *Some* on the pretty petals spills' (p.14). The warrior rejects the boy's advances and breaks away abruptly to obey the bugle-calls summoning him to an approaching battle. A young girl, Mary, who has been watching the scene (presumably gaining from it, as Chubb would have done, a vicarious excitement), now approaches the boy and succeeds in seducing him by the not very original ruse of offering him an apple. The battle rages; the boy dies in the action nestled against the slaughtered body of his beloved warrior. Mary is left alive to bear the boy's child, thereby propagating the race of men-children so recently depleted by the holocaust.

In February of the following year, Chubb began work on a longer poem, this time in blank verse, finally to be called *The Book of God's Madness* but partially published in 1927 as *The Cloud and the Voice.* It is, however, the final version which interests us, for it is in this poem that he declares his philosophy and begins to enlarge on his paederastic inclinations. His philosophy he defines thus:

> This poem—rough fragment though it be—is designed to expose, by satire, the silliness of those who seek a material explanation of the universe; also, by a reduction to absurdity, the error of those who make a god of themselves...Existence, besides being a miracle, is a symbol. Albeit here for inscrutable purposes the spirit is only to be discerned as it were in a distorting-glass.

In a Foreword included in only five copies of the edition of *The Book of God's Madness,* he speaks frankly to his readers. Too long has he lived among women-folk: 'Now I will again seek my chosen lover-comrades, bearded men and rough ungrown youths and lovely-bodied wild-eyed boys adventurous wicked.' In the poem itself he argues for the superiority of Uranian passions:

> Delicious form of youth I love your view,
> Your feel, your sound, your scent, your taste, your all -
>
> I speak to women. –Here behold your king!
>
> The love of man and youth is as two fires,
> Of mother and son two strong and gentle streams,
> The love of man and maid a sluggish rill.

Songs of Mankind, the final book to be printed commercially for Chubb, published in 1930, the year after his literary future was made clear to him, is a far more powerful and uninhibited volume than its predecessors, a collection of verse illustrated with erotic wood engravings. In a wild, prophetic poem, 'Song of My Soul,' he howls his homage to the boys of his dreams:

O burning tongue and hot lips of me explore my love!
Lave his throat with the bubbling fountain of my verse!
Drench him! Slake his loins with it, most eloquent!
Leave no part, no crevice unexplored; delve deep, my minstrel tongue!

For eight years, between 1921 and 1929, Chubb had experimented with many art-forms: oil and watercolour painting; poetry, prose; pencil sketches, woodcuts; hand-presses and commercial printers. In 1929, the turning-point of his literary career, he produced two experiments which shaped his future method of book production. He wrote out *An Appendix*, a notebook of thoughts and ideas which he had jotted down during the war, and laboriously ran off fifty copies on a hand-duplicating machine. He also began work on his illuminated manuscript, *The Book of Visions of Nature and Supernature Solar and Lunar*. He had also been reading William Blake whose technique of book production, the blending of text and illustration rather than the method of printing, for Blake did not use lithography, suited Chubb well, not only for the artistic technique but for conveying similar prophetic utterances. Had Blake not also been a prophet Chubb might not have thought of imitating his *mise-en-page*, but by 1929 Chubb was assured of his own prophetic future. 'I am here to save England; and my spirit shall not rest until the swine of Commerce are driven over the cliffs of Dover,' he writes in *An Appendix*. Chubb had probably drawn some profitable influence from Carpenter's *Towards Democracy*, in which he may well have noted that author's advocation of paederasty. 'Of just such love am I the apostle and forerunner,' he confesses inaccurately, unaware of the Uranian movement which was then just drawing to its close. Both Whitman and Carpenter are imitated in this passage from *The Heavenly Cupid*, the second of the lithographic books:

Outcasts, scrofulous, vicious, virtuous, orthodox, conventional, Ugly and beautiful, I have known them all and respected them; A convict escaped, a burglar of sixteen, a manslayer confess'd, The prostitute girl, the boy of the streets...Trusting them all to the full and never once betrayed.

A little further reading would have led Chubb to the work of many of his contemporaries on the question of paederasty, and had he reached out to grasp the hand of A. T. Bartholomew who wrote to him that year, he would have learned of the existence of several similar minds. Bartholomew had been sent the catalogue of Chubb's watercolours at the Goupil Gallery and had read the controversial penultimate paragraph of the four-page *Note* Chubb had had printed for insertion in the catalogue. It read:

> One thing more, I am unashamed of my body (though very much ashamed of tailors' clothes). I believe absolutely in masculine love–boy-love in particular–of which I claim to be an apostle and forerunner. Let prudes and puritans unknowingly worship Satan in their degree; they will find their mistake, for no man can base his life upon a negation. David and Jonathan, Harmodius and Aristogeiton, Christ and the youthful John, Plato, Socrates, Michelangelo, and Shakespeare are company good enough for me.[4]

Bartholomew knew several Uranian poets, and he would undoubtedly have introduced Chubb to them had he responded to Bartholomew's letter of admiration for the sentiments Chubb had expressed in his note on his paintings:

9 Millington Road
Cambridge
Nov. 20, 1929

Dear Mr Chubb,
Many thanks for your letter of Nov. 10 & now for your further note & the poem, I am very glad to have the little book. I read it when it came to the [Cambridge] University Library & it was that poem chiefly & one or two reproductions of your work which made me feel that I should like to know more about you & your work. It was a great pity that I unavoidably missed your show in London–But some day I hope I shall have the chance of seeing your work (& you) at home–which I should much prefer to a gallery meeting. I agree with almost all that you say in the preface to your catalogue which you sent and especially in the last paragraph but one–which, by the way, is doubtless what gave the Goupil people a fright!...
I am,
Yours sincerely,
A.T.Bartholomew

Chubb was not to be drawn, nor cared to believe that other minds worked along the same paths as his. He also decided to cut himself off from painting ('friends claim more for me as a painter. But this from self-knowledge I repudiate,' he says in *An Appendix*) and from any orthodox method of printing resulting in a wide circulation, in order to indulge his fantasies on the lithographer's stone and to build them into an enormous mystical message for mankind. But few men could afford the expensive folios, as Chubb well knew, and it seems, if truth be told, that he wrote, printed, and published to indulge himself in the exercises of his set symbols, the group of nude boys, his unrequited love for the choir-boy, his involvement in the blacksmith's son's death, and his only active sexual experience, without really caring whether anyone read him or not. Only on these few obsessions could he build his books. With the limitation of his artistic horizon came also a limitation of imagination; only variants and ramifications of these few important events were allowed a place on his pages.

Between 1930 and the outbreak of the Second World War he produced four lithographic works: *The Sun Spirit* (1930), which we have already discussed; *The Heavenly Cupid* (1934); *Water-Cherubs* (1937); and *The Secret Country* (1939). In all of them he formulates his fantasies and attempts to raise his erotic inclinations to a spiritual level. He pours out his longing to join the throng of naked boys he saw so long ago and was only once able to imitate as he coupled with his adolescent lover, and the accompanying lithographs, showing such adolescents under yellow suns and azure skies, lying and leaping on the brightest of green grasses by the silveriest of sequestered streams, underline this yearning to return to the blissful state of pubescent eroticism with his young friend:

> The green green hills, the blue blue sky, blue sea, great golden SUN, yellow dandelions, the pink naked beauty of ripe boyhood, deathless free and happy, brimming with health. This I must have. Nothing less than this can ever satisfy me! GIVE ME MY HEAVEN! GIVE ME MY HEAVEN! *(Water-Cherubs)*

By 1934 he has slightly adapted one of his fixations and retails the new version both in verse and prose in *The Heavenly Cupid*. Whereas before he merely desired to peep at the naked swimmers, now he imagines he chases them through rushes, catches one laggard, forces him to reveal the where-abouts of the others who have managed to hide from him. The boy points to a haystack and Chubb digs in the hay to uncover a 'heaving, tawny mass of boy-flesh' in ecstatic sexual play.

His love of boys, he warns us, must not be underestimated:

> Now, if anyone should suppose that I have exaggerated my love for the bonny darlings, I assure him, or her, that I have mildly understated it. My love for them is so tremendous, so tender, so inexpressible, that if the whole Universe visible and invisible were ranged against it, I should maintain it alone and unsupported for ever. For my pretty cherubs–and for them only–I would brave earth and heaven and hell in league, and vanquish them all.*(Water-Cherubs)*

Sometimes his eroticism is tinged with sadism. Pain and death involving boys fascinate him. In *An Appendix* he describes watching a bout between two boy boxers and his excitement at the thought that he is to sleep, that night, with the bruised and battered loser. In *The Secret Country,* part of which is a prose version of the walking-trip described in the unpublished poem 'The Ballad of the Forest,' a gypsy-boy suggests that Chubb tie him to a tree and whip him. Chubb demurs but in retrospect regrets that he did not accept the invitation for he feels sure both partners would have enjoyed the experience. In *The Heavenly Cupid,* he varies the theme of the early *Sacrifice of Youth* in a poem which treats of the beating to death of a young Spartan in a form of ritual sacrifice.

His basic physical type is a mischievous village boy of small education. 'Alfie's Tale', a story included in *Water-Cherubs,* is an important example of this for it retails the incident of little Alfie who sleeps with an old hermit with the full consent of his mother. Likewise 'Boys on the Quay' (in *The Heavenly Cupid*) describes a boy who seduces him briefly but passionately below a bridge and then tells Chubb of his life on board ship where he found himself the object of two sailors' passion who fight to the death to secure the boy's favours.

Alas, all his stories of erotic encounters are only a dream. In *The Heavenly Cupid*, he writes:

> But O my dream so vivid, mysterious glimpse elusive,
> When youthful naked without blemish I in perfect freedom
> Have met my darling play-mates of delight,
> Down the deep grove thro' which the river runs!
> O ache of my heart upon awakening!
> O ache, ache, ache of my heart.

He realizes he can never enact his desires:

> Who has, at times, not felt it stir?-
> Something masculinely rude,
> Yet 'tis infinitely refin'd,
> Stimulus, yearning, a desire
> To grasp what grasp no mortal could,
> To woo what man ne'er won that woo'd
> To gain what never yet was gain'd! (*The Heavenly Cupid*)

Once only, in *Water-Cherubs,* does Chubb grasp what it is which was certainly driving him on. Is his love for boys, he asks himself, 'simply my own boyish desire, still thirsting for its impossible fulfilment?' This idea, probably more self-revealing than any other of his statements, showed him too poignantly the negation of his dreams and the brief, startlingly frank admission of the sterility of his longings must be immediately suppressed. His philosophy must not be recognized for an erotic introspection conjured from a prurient stunted imagination. Such insight must be eschewed for it allowed no development, and the work in hand of raising his crude, immature sexuality to the stature of a visionary experience must be continued. Therefore the naked adolescent, coarse and unaware of Chubb's doting glances, can in dreams become a god and Chubb undertake his chosen role of the prophet appointed by divine command to herald the Third Dispensation:

> I announce a secret event as tremendous and mysterious as any that has occurred in the spiritual history of the world. I announce the inauguration of

a Third Dispensation, the dispensation of the Holy Ghost on earth, and the
visible advent thereof on earth in the form of a Young Boy of thirteen years
old, naked perfect and unblemished. (*The Heavenly Cupid*)

This spiritualization of paederasty absolves him from the guilt which
makes him hate society and turn into a recluse. His is no longer a common
human weakness, for he has felt the cleansing fire of divinity. In him there
rests something which makes him a unique example of the fusion of the male
and female principles, an androgynic harbinger of Divine Paederasty. Thus
his argument in *The Heavenly Cupid*, but by the time he issued *Water-
Cherubs* it is dismissed as false. Now he is convinced that all feminine
elements are deceptive:

My God was angry with me over those 'bisexual' beings and chastened me
severely. 'I chose you out', He said. 'I gave you male-to-male, youthful! Dare
not to theorize nor follow others' leadings! I bade you Stand Alone, Be
Unafraid! See! Am I not a Boy, All Boy-the Son of My Mother-Boy through
and through, for ever?'

More and more Chubb brooded over the occult significance of his
visions until he saw himself as Raf, the guardian angel of Albion, 'buried
amidst the woodland maze of Pharaoh (or, as it is call'd in its shrunken mortal
counterpart in the world of illusion and shadow, Fairoak)' (*The Child of
Dawn*). He is 'the Child of the Fishes' who will build a school for boys under
the age of fourteen where they will live naked under a vow of silence,
imbibing the divine wisdom taught to them by himself and a few chosen
helpers under a form of anarchical divine government (*The Child of Dawn*).
The heterogeneous mass of occult facts and figures collected in his two post-
war books, *The Child of Dawn* and *Flames of Sunrise*, embraces numerology,
astrology, classical and Celtic mythology, Christianity, the Grail legend, the
works of Paracelsus (which he had recently read), and all these various
systems are twisted and entwined to shed light on his prophecy of the Third
Dispensation, the Advent of the Boy-God. Coincidental dates and minor
chance occurrences are interpreted as auguries of his mission. Along with his
crazed, muddled arguments (on one page-spread alone are sections entitled
'Albion, Isle of Faery', 'The Nine Muses and the Age of Music', 'Priest, King,
Prophet; and the Fiery Baptism', 'The Castle of Carbonek', 'Holly and
Mistletoe', 'The Return of the Children of Promise', and 'The Divine
Trinity') came a disintegration of his handwriting into loops and whorls, the
ascenders and descenders trailing uncontrolled into the lines above and
below, and the crossbars of the t's curving high above the line. Fussy little
decorations and vignettes are inserted at random in the text. Full-page
illustrations are still to be found in as much profusion as in his pre-war books,
the boys and the sequestered streams are still there, but the spaciousness and

light have gone. Now the streams meander through lands thickly wooded with gnarled, knotted trees above which tower enormous mountains, their slopes cluttered with complicated structures of castles, mosques, chapels, in every architectural style. Dragons flit across moonlit skies. Bright haloed *putti*, rayed with astral light, float in the heavens. Even the boys' figures and faces have changed from his earlier portraits. Gone are the slim, dark almond-eyed sylphs of the pre-war years and to replace them are blond, curly-haired, tough, over-developed adolescents with exaggerated pectorals, bicepses and buttocks, similar to the disproportionate drawings in some male-model magazines.

It is possible that the Second World War brought on a recurrence of Chubb's neurasthenia, for *The Child of Dawn* on which he was working in the forties certainly gives an undisciplined, manic impression to a reader. While working on it Chubb tells us, he was already applying himself in a fever of inspiration to the Book of Rapha, which was eventually printed in *Flames of Sunrise*, the idea flooding into his soul with brilliant illumination like the sacred flame that burns for ever in the Holy of Holies, compelling him to further utterance. Thus *Flames of Sunrise* continues his arcane posturings. His identification with the archangel Raphael attracted the attention of the Lord Abbot of the Order of St Raphael, Count Richard Jean Chrétien de Palatine (otherwise known as Ronald Powell), who sent him an illuminated scroll from the Order as an appreciation of his services to mankind. This Order of St Raphael aspired to establish a co-operative movement 'made up of all people who are interested in TRUTH, irrespective of race, colour, creed, or sect; based upon the pattern of the United Nations Organization.'[5] It is not known whether the lord Abbot was gracious enough to confer on Chubb the degrees of the *Université Philotechnique Internationale* of 11 Old Bond Street, with which it has been stated that de Palatine was connected,[6] or whether Chubb was charged the regular retail price of thirty-eight pounds for the bestowal of such an honour.[7]

Even when *Flames of Sunrise* was still on the stone, Chubb, for the first time, faced bravely his disillusionment. In *Treasure Trove*, the book which succeeds it, he notes this:

Alas for blighted hopes and thwarted promise, for the seed of native genius denied its rightful growth to harvest and fruition, by a cold and callous world! Forty years followed of frustration and disillusionment–forty years 'in the wilderness', over which it is happier to draw a veil.

A failed prophet, he despairingly cast his eye over the unsold folios and quartos, the watercolours and designs, and feverishly began to pack parcels of them for despatch, gratis, to libraries and art-galleries. In his search through his belongings he came across a sheaf of manuscripts of fairy-tales that he had written in childhood and early youth. He remembered, too, his love for the illustrations of Gustave Doré and it is Doré's influence which is obvious in the plates of *Treasure Trove* and his final book, *The Golden City*, which contain the lithographed text of this childish story-telling. Chubb's childhood might have vanished, the memories of it have played him false, but these boyish manuscripts proved to him the reality of that long-past time, and their asexual medieval imagery provided a secure haven for the failed but unembittered prophet.

5

'Dr Trelawney' and Aleister Crowley

ONE of the many periodically recurrent characters in Anthony Powell's novel-sequence, *A Dance to the Music of Time* (1951-1975) is Dr Trelawney, thaumaturge and seer. Introduced at first as a harmless eccentric, he is revealed in due course to be one of the most significant figures in the action. Despite his appearing only twice 'on stage'– confrontations, that is, with the narrator, Nicholas Jenkins–his teachings are disquieteningly pervasive, touching on the lives of many of the other personages, Giles Jenkins, Mrs Erdleigh, Hugh Moreland, General Conyers, Canon Fenneau, and, most importantly, Scorpio Murtlock, whose revival of Dr Trelawney's 'cult' will lead the archetypal Kenneth Widmerpool to madness and, finally, to his death.

There are reasons to suggest that Dr Trelawney is modelled on Aleister (b. Edward Alexander) Crowley (1875-1947), himself thaumaturge and seer, whose life and doctrines were regularly given disadvantageous airings in the British press in the twenties and thirties; and these notes seek to show that Powell, who had met Crowley and who had learned of his reputation from a woman friend, rather a victim, of the magician, has employed his knowledge of Crowley's activities and philosophies to flesh out one of the more intriguing characters in the interlinking series of novels that span life in Britain from 1914 to 1971.

Trelawney first crosses the path of the narrator in 1914 when he (Jenkins) is still a boy of seven or eight, a period of life he reconstructs in *The Kindly Ones* from the distance of some quarter of a century. Trelawney is already running a cult. Robed disciples, headed by their master are to been seen every so often on runs through the heathland of the area of Hampshire where Nicholas's parents are resident. Crowley had formed his magical cult, the A∴ A∴, in 1907 and by 1914 had for two years been concerned with the promotion of another one, the M∴M∴M∴, its teachings based on sexual practices–other doctrines roughly consonant with the already established fraternity–and although disciples did not, like Dr Trelawney's, live under one roof, Crowley, as we know from a manifesto issued in about 1913, envisaged the possibility of their doing so. Crowley's followers, although not required to run, were subjected to other physical disciplinary ordeals of a more uncomfortable nature–the razor-slashing of a forearm, for instance, to increase verbal vigilance–and Powell's invention of running has been derived from knowledge of these disciplines or from the fact that Crowley was a keen walker and mountaineer.

Nicholas's mother, whom Dr Trelawney profoundly disturbs, encounters him in the local post-office where she hears him utter his watchword, 'The Essence of the All is the Godhead of the True', to which initiates were expected to respond with an equally sacred and enigmatic catchphrase, 'The Vision of Visions heals the Blindness of Sight'. Like Trelawney, Crowley too demanded such a spiritual interchange before conversation of any kind, spiritual or otherwise, got under way. Synthesis of *The Book of the Law,* his most important hieratic text, supernaturally (he claimed) delivered at Cairo in 1904 and the foundation of his life's work, the phrase was habitually employed as a written and a verbal greeting: 'Do what thou wilt shall be the whole of the Law.' The correct response was: 'Love is the Law, Love under Will.'

The Book of the Law was printed several times, its author–more correctly the vehicle for its transmission–proclaiming that publication set in motion, after a statutory nine-month gestation period, some world-shattering event, its third printing in 1914 precipitating the First World War and the eighth in 1938 the second. In 1939, at Nicholas's second meeting with Dr Trelawney–his first as an adult–the seer predicts the impending holocaust: 'The sword of Mithras, who each year immolates the sacred bull, will ere long flash from its scabbard' (*The Kindly Ones*) and, in retrospect, as Hilary Spurling points out in her handbook to *A Dance*, because Nicholas's first encounter with the Doctor was just prior to the Great War, he can be looked upon as a harbinger of both conflicts.

Physically, Dr Trelawney does not much resemble Crowley to begin with–silky beard, long hair, uncomfortably Biblical air–but then photographs of the young and middle-aged Crowley are so dissimilar–contingent perhaps upon the sort of unease with progress that requires adoption of ever-changing personae–as to cause hesitation that one is examining the same set of features; nor were Powell's autobiographical records of Crowley encountered over a lunch table incorporated into Dr Trelawney's portrait: 'big, weary-looking...with an unusual formation of a bald and shaven skull,' nor a later glimpse of him in Great Ormond Street, 'hatless, heavily bespectacled...dressed in green plus fours'. In 1939, however, appearances of Trelawney, on his way out, and of Crowley, equally decrepit, are quite similar:

> Even the beard, straggling, dirty grey, stained yellow in places like the patches of broom on the common beyond Stonehurst, had lost all resemblance to that worn by the athletic, vigorous prophet of those distant days. Once broad and luxuriant, it was now shrivelled almost to a goatee. He no longer seemed to have stepped down from a stained-glass window or ikon. His skin was dry and blotched. Dark spectacles covered his eyes, his dressing-gown a long blue oriental robe that swept the ground. He really looked rather frightening (*The Kindly Ones*).

This description may be a synthesis of two Crowley likenesses dating from his last years when he, like Dr Trelawney, was living in a seaside boarding-house, a snapshot reproduced in his biography, *The Great Beast* by John Symonds (1951), which shows the beard and a dark garment of some kind, and a pencil drawing by Augustus John which depicts him with wildly staring eyes. Powell may have seen that reproduced as the frontispiece to Crowley's selected poems, *Olla* (1946), or, since they were acquainted– Powell sitting to John in 1960–seen the original at the artist's studio.

The first direct encounter with Trelawney as opposed to the heathland sightings takes place at the end of a trying day for Nicholas's parents.

They have invited to lunch General Aylmer Conyers, friend of Nicholas's grandparents and a distant cousin of his mother, together with Conyers's wife. It was the day the parlour-maid, Billson, never absolutely steady-minded, had taken it into her head to appear naked in the drawing-room, on top of which, without suitable warning or exact notice of time of arrival, Giles Jenkins, Nicholas's egregious and financially shaky uncle, had proposed himself for a visit of unspecified length. General Conyers has shown great presence of mind and kindness of heart over the Billson episode and the Jenkins's are waving him goodbye when he nearly runs his car into Dr Trelawney and his party who suddenly break cover on one of their runs. To the Jenkins's surprise, the two are acquainted, the General answering Trelawney's password with the correct occult corollary. Crowley too had a military follower, in fact only a captain at the time of his allegiance but in later life nearing the rank of General Conyers: Major-General J. F. C. Fuller. This fact was also known to Powell who records quite correctly in his autobiography that Fuller wrote an exegesis on Crowley's philosophies entitled *The Star in the West* (1907).

During the ensuing conversation with the General, Dr Trelawney, suggesting 'a rhythmical month under instruction', assures him nothing too strenuous need be undertaken: 'You would be subjected to none but probationary exercises at first. Disciplines of the Adept would not be expected of you in the early days' (*The Kindly Ones*). These hints at some sort of hierarchical structure to Dr Trelawney's order are borne out in reality, Crowley subdividing standards of prowess into eleven grades, Probationer–Dr Trelawney's proposed level of work for General Conyers–the lowest rung on the ladder.

Conyers is far from averse, in principle, to making a retreat, pleading only current commitments as reason for not then and there joining up. 'Give me a change of routine,' he says. 'Got very interested in such things in India. *Bodhisattvas* and such like, *Mahasatipatthana* and all that reflection.' The two Buddhist references, the first to a Buddha who elects to remain corporeally embodied to aid others on the Path, the second a form of meditative self-enquiry–a 'reflection' as the General quite correctly perceives it–find their place in Crowleyan ethics. Buddhist texts were 'officially approved' by the A∴A∴ for study by neophytes and Crowley's Liber XIV in *The Book of Lies* (1913) was an improvement, as he saw it, on the Eastern method of self-analysis.

Jenkins's reminiscences of Trelawney, dating from 1914, are in fact recorded in 1939 prompted by talks about their childhood with his musical friend, Hugh Moreland, who then sketches in for Nicholas Trelawney's career to date:

'I used to hear about Trelawney long before I met him,' Moreland said.'One of the down-at-heel poets we knew was a friend of his-indeed, the two of them were said to have enjoyed the favours of succubi together on the Astral Plane...What was more exciting, my aunt knew a girl who–to use her own phrase-fell into his clutches...she cast herself from a Welsh mountain-top-Trelawney had a kind of temple at that time in a remote farmhouse in North Wales. There was quite a scandal. He was attacked in one of the Sunday papers...There was talk of nameless rites, drugs, disagreeable forms of discipline (*The Kindly Ones*).

Moreland's 'seedy poet' has his counterpart in Victor Benjamin Neuburg (1883-1940), not an altogether forgettable character, especially to be admired for his furtherance of the career of Dylan Thomas. While not in fact 'enjoying the favours of succubi', he and Crowley performed two important magical rituals, a more or less 'classical' one in North Africa in 1909, and another, based on Crowley's sex-teachings, in Paris in 1914. If one transfers the Welsh farmhouse to one in Cefalù, Sicily, substitutes a male disciple, Raoul Loveday, for the girl, and accidental death for suicide–'nameless rites, drugs, disagreeable forms of discipline' allowed to stand as more or less correct description of day-to-day life in Crowley's 'Abbey'–this chapter of Trelawney's life finds its parallel in Crowley's own in the period 1920-23.

Moreland then delivers a throwaway remark on his own magical interests but, in doing so, lays the basis for one of the more remarkable allusions in *Dance*: 'My own occult interests are so sketchy. I've just thumbed through *Dogme et Rituel de la Haute Magie.*' Moreland's dalliance with an arcane text by a French ex-prelate, Alphonse Louis Constant (1810-1875), calling himself Eliphas Levi, is of enormous significance since Crowley believed himself to be Levi reincarnated and incorporated much of the book's teachings into his own scheme of things. Crowley learned his magic in a group known as the Hermetic Order of the Golden Dawn (W. B. Yeats was a member) who paid due attention to the panoply of the Egyptian gods (Dr Trelawney refers to Seth, or at least to the 'Slayer of Osiris') whose worship Levi also held in high esteem. In *Dogme et Rituel*–to sustain Moreland's rather pretentious referral to the original French although a readily available English translation is far more likely his source–Levi expounds on the symbolism of the Sphinx. She–rather 'it', Levi propounding hermaphroditic qualities–has four distinct aspects, man, lion, eagle, bull, themselves attributable to the four 'fixed' signs of the zodiac, Aquarius, Leo, Scorpio, Taurus, and to the four elements, air, fire, water, earth; a synthesis, therefore, of the universe itself. Levi further assigns four precepts to his four sub-divisions of the Egyptian glyph, prerequisites, he states, of magical attainment:

> To attain the SANCTUM REGNUM, in other words, the knowledge and power of the Magi, there are four indispensable conditions–an intelligence illuminated by study, an intrepidity which nothing can check, a will which cannot be broken, and a prudence which nothing can corrupt and nothing intoxicate. TO KNOW, TO DARE, TO WILL, TO KEEP SILENCE–such are the four worlds of the Magus, inscribed upon the four symbolical forms of the Sphinx (*Transcendental Magic* tr. A. E. Waite.)

These technicalities Powell has perfectly assimilated because, in the second confrontation between Nicholas and Trelawney–considerably aged, locked in an hotel bathroom, deprived of heroin–he makes him remark to the worldly Bob Duport, keen only to make money, anxious as he tells Trelawney 'to shake the metal market': 'To know, to will, to dare, to keep silent, those are the things required' (*The Kindly Ones*).

Albert Creech, owner of the hotel in whose bathroom Dr Trelawney has found himself incarcerated, not anticipating Nicholas's and Bob Duport's assistance in freeing his eccentric guest, has sent for a companion of Trelawney's, Mrs Erdleigh. Originally introduced in *The Acceptance World* as cartomancer, planchette manipulator–only that far magically advanced– she will re-echo Levi's precepts to Odo Stevens during an air-raid:

'Any last words of advice, Mrs Erdleigh?' asked Stevens. He treated her as if he were consulting the Oracle at Delphi. 'Let the palimpsest of your mind absorb the words of Eliphas Levi–to know, to will, to dare, to be silent' (*The Military Philosophers*).

Trelawney dies not long after the outbreak of war: not so his creeds. Those, it comes to Nicholas's attention, have been revived by the distinctly sinister–more so, in some ways, than their originator–Scorpio Murtlock, who makes his bow in the final volume of the sequence, *Hearing Secret Harmonies*. We are now in 1968. Murtlock, son, as was Crowley, of fanatically religious parents (Plymouth Brethren in Crowley's case), is reputed to have tendencies towards his own sex (Crowley too, although only for magical purposes). Significantly born under one of Levi's 'fixed' zodiacal signs, he can be accounted a 'hippie'–rootlessness at any rate proposed by his living in a caravan when he comes into Nicholas's life, presence at Stonehenge with similarly vagrant camp-followers, homelessness circumvented only by his taking over Widmerpool's place at Stourwater–and the hippie movement in real life saw an upsurge of interest in Crowley's teachings. Nicholas learns much of Murtlock's equivocal past from another shady figure, encountered at a Royal Academy dinner, Canon Paul Fenneau. Here again Crowleyan connections subsist because Fenneau seems likely to be a pen-portrait of the real life demonologist, the Rev Montague Summers (1880-1948). Fenneau and Trelawney turn out to have been acquainted despite divergent trains of thought and occult standpoints and appear to have treated each other with respect. Crowley and Summers were of a kind, Summers attacking Crowley's mystique as 'all filth and wickedness' in one of his many histories of witchcraft, Crowley recording in his diary some years before that he had spent a very pleasant evening in Summers's company. Powell may not have met Summers–he does not mention him in his autobiography–and the portrait of Fenneau may be derived from a novel by Dennis Wheatley, *To the Devil a Daughter* (1953), into which Powell may have dipped for the more lurid, the more satanic, aspects of Trelawney's art at which the doctor hints in *The Kindly Ones*, 'those phantasms of the incubi that rack the dreams of young girls, or the libidinous gymnastics of the goat-god whose ice-cold sperm fathers monsters on writhing witches in covens.' In Wheatley's novel, there is a Canon Copely-Syle, 'plump both in face and figure. His cheeks were rosy but tended to sag a little; the rest of his skin had such a childlike pinkness that it was difficult to visualize him ever having the need to shave. His forehead was broad and smooth; his long silver hair swept back from it to fall in curls on the nape of his neck...His eyes were hazel, but very pale, and his expression benign.' Fenneau is described as 'smooth, plump, grey curls (...in neat waves)...small eyes...the main feature. They were unusual eyes, not only almost unnaturally small, but vague, moist, dreamy, the eyes of a medium. The cherubic side, increased by a long slightly uptilted nose, was a little too good to be true.' Both descriptions fit Montague Summers.

Things develop more along Summers's lines of research from this point, witchcraft more than Crowley's intellectual occultism now much to the fore. A masked naked dance is held among the cultists to raise the spirit of Dr Trelawney, sexual coupling part of the nocturnal rite. An American professor, Russell Gwinnett, describes the scene to Nicholas:

> 'Scorp said that–among the ones taking part in the rite–they should have been all with all, each with each, within the sacred circle. I was a short way apart. Not in the circle. Scorp thought that best.'
>
> Gwinnett again put up his hand to his head. He looked as if he might faint. Then he seemed to recover himself. Heavy spots of rain were beginning to fall.
>
> 'Did everyone in the circle achieve sexual relations with everyone else?'
>
> 'If they could.'
>
> 'Were they all up to it?'
>
> 'Only Scorp.'
>
> 'He must be a remarkable young man.'
>
> 'It wasn't for pleasure. This was an invocation.'

Powell has not entirely deserted Crowleyan propositions. His second magical order, the M∴M∴M∴, advocated sexual practices, though not for pleasure either. The partner–sex unimportant, for preference not an initiate– is used for invocationary purposes. The moment of orgasm is sacred, its fluidic products sacramental. Psychic attunement at that moment should be on the occult task in hand. These matters are hinted at in Crowley's standard text, *Magick in Theory and Practice,* the book reviled by Summers who misinterprets sexual oblations for immolatory ones.

The sequence of *Dance* ends in 1971: continuance of Dr Trelawney's cult, now Widmerpool is dead, Scorpio Murtlock's sole preserve, Powell leaves us believing is assured, a prediction borne out in fact. Crowley's followers indeed proliferate, practise the rites, publish books, accept probationers. British enthusiasts, propagating beliefs mainly in mimeographed magazine format–*Kaos, The Lamp of Thoth, Ganymede, Nuit-Isis, Daath Papers, Starfire*–abound. Dr Trelawney's prediction seems to have been fulfilled: 'There is no death in Nature, only transition, blending, synthesis, mutation' (*The Military Philosophers*). Less occultly, though still a matter for speculation, that tenet underpins Powell's own thesis, the bedrock on which the series of novels is based:

> Mummers return, who might have been supposed to have made their final exit...The touching-up of time-expired sets, reshaping of derelict props, updating of old refrains, are none of them uncommon.

6
'Pregnant with Mandrakes'
Florence Farr

FLORENCE FARR (1860-1917) was the youngest, very much the youngest, of the five children of William Farr, a colleague of Florence Nightingale (in whose memory he presumably named his youngest child), a man who combined a talent for medicine with a genius for statistics. The death of Florence's mother when she was sixteen and of her father seven years later gave her an early if involuntary foretaste of the emancipation that satisfied her so much in adulthood. She continued her education, regularly at first, then less so, finally giving it up altogether. For a short while she became a teacher under the delusion, still common today, that those whose formal studies have been abandoned or performed without noticeable merit are better prepared to instruct the young than qualified scholars. Her aspirations then turned to the stage, an arena where her talent and her beauty procured her fame and love and led her into the occult society that was the inspiration for her book *Egyptian Magic.*

Florence was a woman of many parts, eager to learn and to distribute the fruits of her learning. W. B. Yeats compared her mind with the game of spillikins, a bundle of different coloured sticks all muddled together. With Florence you never knew which coloured stick of knowledge she would suddenly withdraw from her sheaf. Ezra Pound, who met Florence in America with the philanthrophist John Quinn, observed the same thing:

> One comes to you
> And takes strange gain away:

Trophies fished up; some curious suggestion;
Fact that leads nowhere; and a tale or two
Pregnant with mandrakes...

She was musical, musical enough to tour America with Arnold Dolmetsch where she spoke verse to Dolmetsch's accompaniment on a specially designed psaltery–an evening's entertainment that one cannot help feeling did not always play to packed houses–although Dolmetsch had considerable reservations about her talent. She learned embroidery from William Morris's daughter, May. She wrote a novel, some plays reflecting her fascination with ancient Egypt, and a book on female emancipation, her brief marriage to Edward Emery, one of the famous family of actors, having convinced her of the boredom of household drudgeries and the tiresomeness, not to say actual detestation, of physical love when unaccompanied by mutual admiration.

She had a certain administrative capacity, evidenced by her managership of the Avenue Theatre, her position as Scribe in the Order of the Golden Dawn, and her eventual assumption of the principalship of a girls' school in Ceylon, but her incorrigibly 'flighty' attitude to affairs of the heart spilled over into her everyday life. Her talent on the stage never rose to genius; her musical ability remained second rate, and there were grave faults in her managerial duties at the Golden Dawn headquarters. Her letters from Ceylon too, exhibit her inherent laziness and she speaks, not of the workaday problems of superintending a boarding school in a foreign land, but of her idyllic existence, and of the exotic odour she exuded owing to her consumption twice a day of spicy curries.

There remained, always, her charm and her beauty, 'her large eyes and crescent eyebrows and a smile', and her 'spillikins' of knowledge on which she could draw to entertain and attract her audience. If someone wanted to talk spooks, she would talk them; if they turned the conversation to music or the theatre, she was ready for them. Furthermore, if a man wanted to make love to her, that, too, came very easily. By 1894 she had, according to George Bernard Shaw, a list of fourteen lovers.

Shaw and Yeats came into her life at much the same time, in 1890, at Bedford Park, a red-brick London suburb teeming with cockroaches and Bohemians not far from where she had lived with her unsatisfactory husband from whom, now, she had been separated for two years without troubling to instigate divorce proceedings. Coincidentally, several Golden Dawn members lived there and coincidentally again, although occultists would not say so, there is still a Golden Dawn tradition in Bedford Park. The Yeats family had come to London from Ireland (for the second time) in 1887 and had moved to Bedford Park, perhaps to be near the Morris family who lived in Hammersmith, the following year. Yeats saw Florence in a play, *A Sicilian*

Idyll, written by an Irish doctor, John Todhunter, who 'looked exactly like God in an illustrated family Bible,' and much admired her rendering of the verse. They were drawn together by a mutual interest in the occult. Florence, like Yeats, had been studying such matters for some time, certainly for ten years, since she noted, on quitting her education, that her horoscope was auspicious for such a decision. Yeats had begun with Theosophy, a cult that was sweeping England, appealing not only to the genuine seeker but also to the fashionably giddy and empty headed as Spiritualism had done some years before; but he was interested in the physical phenomena of mysticism and these, as Madame Blavatsky herself had stated, were not to be found in the Theosophical Society. However, the Society's journal, *Lucifer,* included a veiled reference to another society where such things were being investigated–the Hermetic Order of the Golden Dawn.

Yeats was initiated into the Golden Dawn in March 1890 and introduced Florence later the same year. For both of them advancement in the Order came swiftly. It was the Order, more than anything else, that was the link between them. Whether they were in love with each other is unclear. Yeats's sisters suspected so and Yeats himself records that Florence was the only person in his life to whom he could tell everything. This need not be taken as evidence of any greater intimacy. Probably they had a brief affair, but Florence's insincerity about matters of the heart–at any protestation of affection she was inclined to become 'stagy' and affected–and her rejection of the institution of marriage would, for Yeats, have made it a transitory association. In any case, another woman, Maud Gonne, came into Yeats's life and Florence found herself involved with a man in every way different from Yeats and one who demonstrably did fall in love with her: George Bernard Shaw.

Shaw was among the first-night audience of *A Sicilian Idyll* and was as impressed as Yeats by Florence's talent. He was involved with several other women at the time but was soon seeing Florence every day. He had a fascination for married women and liked to insinuate himself into married households, not really to carry off the bride but to woo her at a distance. He had, too, long been obsessed with the 'emancipated' woman and with a desire to prove to the public that actresses were not habitually loose women but honest, hardworking, people getting on with their careers. To find an emancipated woman who was an actress and, at his instigation, a divorcee, was the fulfillment of several dreams at once. Not that Shaw was a dreamer (as Yeats was): he was a fighter, diligent and high-minded and, regardless of his passion for Florence, he began a ruthless grooming of her as an actress, particularly as an interpreter of the female roles in the plays of Ibsen.

To be fair to Florence, there were good reasons why she accepted, indeed actively encouraged, the attentions of Yeats and Shaw; and, to be fair to them, equally good reasons for their finding her unsatisfactory. She shared with Yeats a fascination for magic, with Shaw a love of the theatre and an ambition, at least the semblance of an ambition, to become a great actress. Yeats, however, disliked her facile mind and her ingrained artificiality, which were probably the attributes, if only they could have been tamed to his liking, that appealed to Shaw. Shaw, in his turn, despised occult pursuits, was appalled by their irrationality. Florence would not, more likely could not, keep silent to Shaw about them. At her home he would have seen her paintings of Egyptian gods and goddesses, although not, it is to be hoped, her magical weapons and temple regalia, and he knew of *Egyptian Magic*: 'You would not believe in my doctrine of working at some reality every day,' he railed at her; 'but you none the less worked every day at your unreality. And now you think to undo the work of all those years by a phrase and a shilling's worth of exoteric Egyptology.' Nevertheless it is hard to believe that Shaw was not thinking a little of Florence when he wrote *Caesar and Cleopatra*.

Shaw and Yeats continued to write parts for her in their plays, Shaw some very fine ones, but a rift was inevitable. Florence felt more for the Golden Dawn than she did for the exhausting hobby-horses Shaw kept badgering her to ride. Shaw knew this perfectly well, sheered off, retrenched elsewhere, blotted her from his mind. In old age he could not even remember having written to her, although several letters survive. Yeats bowed out too, but intellectually the Golden Dawn kept them together. It was the Order that let them down finally, not the other way round. They were both victims of an internecine war they were powerless to oppose.

Florence's *Egyptian Magic,* issued in 1896 over her Golden Dawn motto initials, S.S.D.D. (' Sapientia Sapienti Dona Data': 'Wisdom is given as a gift to the wise') was number 8 of a 9-volume sequence of occult tracts, 'Collectanea Hermetica.' Edited by William Wynn Westcott, head of the Golden Dawn, the series, while not required reading for Order members, is unquestionably doctrinaire. All the Golden Dawn rituals are redolent with Egyptian symbolism and it is with this in mind, together with Florence's insistence on the efficacy of practical magic, that the book must be read. Slight though it may appear today, even a little pretentious in its lengthy translations from Gnostic fragments of which there were after all French versions already in print but included perhaps because of the similarity of some of the 'barbarous names of evocation' to the Enochian language taught to Golden Dawn members, it is nevertheless a pioneering book. The science of Egyptology was only just coming of age. The OED does not record a use of the word before 1859. Although there was, at the time Florence produced her book, a Professorship at London University, it had been established solely for the magisterial Flinders Petrie. There would be no academic foundation at Oxford for another five years and Cambridge would have to wait over a quarter of a century longer. Yet, strangely, it was from Cambridge that the three greatest English Egyptologists came: Charles Wycliffe Goodwin, E. A. Wallis Budge, and Herbert Thompson. Of these, the studies of Wallis Budge were the most important for Florence and for the Golden Dawn, for in 1892 Budge had been appointed Acting Keeper of the Egyptian department in the British Museum, around the corner from the Golden Dawn's London temple, and had been elevated to Principal Keeper in 1894. It is rumoured that he was not unsympathetic to Order pursuits and probably aided members in their researches. Florence would have been proud that her book on Egyptian Magic preceded that of Budge's by two years.

This is not the place to iterate the story of the establishment of the Golden Dawn, its schisms and its eventual demise. That can be found in several other places. Suffice it to say that its foundations, laid on the twin quicksands of a forged charter and an arrogant sacerdotalism, were bound to subside, yet not before there had been recruited into it some splendid and genuine minds: Florence herself, Yeats, Allan Bennett (with whom Florence summoned to visible appearance the spirit of Mercury), the Order's bugbear, Aleister Crowley (who much admired Florence) and its uncanny tutelary genius, Samuel Liddell MacGregor Mathers. In 1897, the Order's founder and the forger of its charter, W. W. Westcott, was rumbled as being a practising magician. As well as having a financial interest in the Sanitary Wood Wool Company—perhaps some precursor to Chilprufe—he was also a Coroner. There was no hint of necromantic practices in the Golden Dawn, but to the unversed minds of Westcott's superiors such a suspicion occurred. As Aleister Crowley pointed out, he was employed to sit on corpses not to raise them and he found it prudent to resign. This left Mathers as Head of the Order, quite rightly so, since he and his clairvoyant wife, the sister of the French philosopher Henri Bergson, had written most of the rituals; but their ill-timed decision to go to live in Paris, from where his autocracy in all Order matters became almost megalomaniacal, left remaining London members with a quantity of pricks against which to kick. Mathers refused to yield his authority to anyone else and expelled several recalcitrant members, Florence, originally his London representative, among them. The London Temple defiantly reconstituted the Order without him and Florence became its Scribe, responsible for various administrative tasks and for examining candidates, but she soon found herself in as much trouble with the new regime as she had been with Mathers. Miss Annie Horniman, who had supported Mathers financially and had put up the money for Florence to produce the season of plays at the Avenue Theatre which had included Yeats's *Land of Heart's Desire* and

Shaw's *Arms and the Man,* disapproved of the somewhat slapdash methods Florence was employing in her duties. Squabbles continued to break out intermittently and eventually Florence resigned.

With hindsight, what is interesting is that the Order does seem to have been established *sub specie aeternitatis.* Its rituals are still performed, its philosophies still much admired. If, as Yeats alleged, there is any truth in 'the practice and philosophy of what we have agreed to call magic, in what I must call the evocation of spirits,' the Golden Dawn system is still the most efficacious; but there must be harmony and a singleness of purpose. To quote Yeats again: 'If we preserve the unity of the Order, if we make that unity efficient among us, the Order will become a single very powerful talisman.' This was not to be. The system demanded a formal, disciplined training with overseers to be respected and laws to be obeyed. It was not founded to be run on the 'progressive' lines of its reconstitution where every member did much as he liked, formed groups within it (as Florence founded one, for the purposes of skrying in the Tree of Life), bent the rules and altered the curriculum. The dangers of such an approach to any educational system are obvious.

If Mathers had stayed put and had displayed the smallest tinge of humility who knows to what heights the Order might have risen; but Florence, at loggerheads with both her original Chief and the new administration, had had enough. Her departure for Ceylon in 1912 can be seen as a symbolic shaking off of the Order's dust from her feet. Her co-magician, Allan Bennett, had made the same journey, for the same reasons, perhaps had even paved the way for her new appointment. Many of her friends begged her not to go, but she would not listen. Yeats particularly mourned her departure and wrote sadly in *A Vision* that she

Preferred to teach a school
Away from neighbour and friend
Among dark skins, and there
Permit foul years to wear
Hidden from eyesight, to the unnoticed end.

7

'You Can't See The Wood For Detritus' The Catalogue of Erotica in the British Library*

DESPITE Mr Legman's conjecture, in his extraordinary introduction to this volume, that the Private Case dates from the receipt in 1866 of the 'phallicism' collection of the antiquarian, George Witt, I would like to suggest that in general 'private' cases of books probably evolve rather than get consciously constructed. Someone, somewhere, a librarian, a parent or a schoolmaster, considers a book politically unsound, theologically heterodox, or just not quite nice, and consigns it to a place where it cannot be consulted. If I may give two microcosmic examples to try to make my point: my nanny's little *'enfer'* consisted of an uncle's substantial run of *London Opinion* and a copy of *Rupert and the Black Dwarf*, each title in its own way being considered too heady for juvenile perusal and placed high out of reach on a child-proof shelf. Likewise, at the circulating library attached to the bookshop where I worked at the time of the publication of Philip Roth's novel on solitary habits, a customer walked in with a copy between finger and thumb and dropped it onto the librarian's desk. 'I don't know about Portnoy,' she remarked, 'but I've got one.' The librarian immediately cast it into one of her drawers (reserved for such purposes and the subject of predictable jokes by the male staff, and there

* Review of Patrick J. Kearney's *The Private Case: An Annotated Bibliography of the Private Case Erotica Collection in the British (Museum) Library*. Introduction by G. Legman

it remained until the library's final closure, when a search of her desk revealed a score of such books condemned over the years by subscribers and by herself, together with an interesting collection of letters relating to the banning of *The Well of Loneliness,* some from the authoress herself.

When such arbitrary censorship is carried out in an institution the size of the British Library, it is remarkable how easily many books, censured by how many eyes, perhaps a few by the great Panizzi himself, can simply vanish, especially since it was the Library's policy not to enter them in the General Catalogue. This sorry state of affairs was brought to light in 1966 with the publication of Peter Fryer's *Private Case–Public Scandal.* As Mr Kearney says in the preface to *The Private Case: An Annotated Bibliography of the Private Case Erotica Collection in the British (Museum) Library,* 'due no doubt at least in part to the agitation by [Mr Fryer] and other workers in the field of erotica and related subjects, a decision was made by the Trustees to incorporate the titles and pressmarks of Private Case (PC) books into the General Catalogue.'

However, because of lack of time or money or a residual puritanism, there is no official catalogue of the Private Case. There was an unofficial attempt at it in 1936 by Alfred Rose writing under the pseudonym of Rolf S. Reade, in that he incorporated in a bibliography of erotica the British Library holdings with their press-marks. But Rose died before publication and his book, insufficiently edited, is a sorry affair. Mr Kearney has now done the Library's duty with a good deal more exuberance than the Trustees would have felt necessary for the task.

Cecil Woolf's remark on the bibliography of Norman Douglas's *Some Limericks* being 'as tangled as an old sewing-basket' is applicable to the whole field of erotica. As in no other sphere of the science, the title-page, the very backbone of a printed book, becomes totally untrustworthy. Let us take Kearney 243 whose title-page reads: 'The Merry Order of St Bridget. Personal Recollections of the Use of the Rod by Margaret Anson. York: Printed for the Author's Friends, 1857.' The author is not Margaret Anson but James G. Bertram, the place of publication is not York but London; the printer may have been John Camden Hotten and the publication date is not 1857 but 1868. At least the title is correct, but even titles have to be carefully watched for they are not always what they seem. *Double Life of Cuthbert Cockerton* (Kearney 1549) turns out to be a translation of Restif de la Bretonne's *Anti-Justine.* And so the 1,920 entries in the catalogue have all had to be subjected to Mr Kearney's scholarly scrutiny in order to arrive, in Mr Legman's words, at 'these difficult-to-come-by bracketed truths,' and wherever possible not only authors but printers and publishers are identified. I can add one snippet of information to Mr Kearney's findings: on the evidence of type-ornaments the printer of Aleister Crowley's *Scented Garden of Abdullah the Satirist* (Kearney 510) is the Parisian firm of Philippe Renouard, then (in 1910) at 19, rue des Saints-Pères. Similar ornaments are used in the same author's *Sword of Song* ('Benares,' 1904) and in his notorious (and not-in-PC) *Snowdrops from a Curate's Garden* [1904?].

This is not a book of tittle-tattle and *on dits*. Following in Mr Legman's spirited and idiosyncratic footsteps, Mr Kearney, firing from both barrels, demolishes pseudonyms like a cowboy smashing bottles in a bar-room, and woven into his staid bibliographical canvas is a host of colourful figures, shorn of their aliases: authors, publishers, illustrators, booksellers, who have had a hand in this bizarre trade almost since the invention of moveable types. Perhaps the strangest of these is Alphonse Momas, a hack-pornographer or *'pisse-copie'* (Mr. Legman's expression), who wrote no fewer than forty-five books in the PC and whose output was so prolific that he had to use nine pseudonyms: Le Nismois, Tap-Tap, Cain d'Abel, L'Erotin, Fuckwell, Un journaliste du siècle dernier, Mercadette, Pan-Pan, and Trix. Mr Kearney tells us Momas was a civil servant attached to the Paris police and that he devoted himself to spiritualism in later life. I recall reading, in some attack on spiritualism, perhaps one of Fr Raupert's spirited diatribes, of a clergyman much given to the practice of automatic writing who, to his distress, found his hand suddenly impelled by an agency capable only of the grossest indecencies. Each day on awakening from the trance into which he had thrown himself, pen in hand, in humble expectation of exploring life beyond the veil, he discovered he had been delivered of page after page of writings of the lowest and most shocking kind. Perhaps it was the spirit of 'Tap-Tap', 'coming through'.

Public libraries find it difficult to justify disbursements of public money for the acquisition of erotic material, fearing the sort of horrified outcry from that portion of the press that emulates–if it does not actually surpass–the literature it is denouncing. At the instigation of Peter Fryer, the BL did actually buy one book (Kearney 923)–one can imagine the trembling of the hand that signed the cheque, the whispered injunctions to secrecy–but has otherwise relied on benefactors for its acquisitions, and Mr Kearney has usefully provided provenances where he can for the books under his notice. By far the largest and most renowned bequest was that of Henry Spencer Ashbee ('Pisanus Fraxi', author of three discursive bibliographical volumes published between 1877 and 1885 whose usefulness Mr Kearney now threatens to topple) received by the BL in 1900, but the next bumper crop did not arrive until 1965 on the death of Charles Reginald Dawes. Dawes, like so many of the characters mentioned by the compiler and his introducer ('Slapsie Maxie', Elias Gaucher, etc) is best described as 'shadowy', but seems to have been a delightful and cultured man, ready to help scholars who wished to examine his fine collection. Judging from his own manuscript fictions which I acquired for a private collector, he had leanings towards homosexuality with a special predilection for the activity described in the title of an erotic playlet by de Maupassant mentioned by Mr Legman in his introduction; but he was refreshingly eclectic in his collecting tastes and his library considerably enriches the Private Case. A few rarities somehow got away, however, including a copy of a scarce novel, *Suburban Souls* (1901), and a book that was floating round the London book-trade shortly after his death, *Memoirs of a Voluptuary* (3 volumes, 1905). Another Dawes item which I bought at auction was one of two copies on vellum of Octave Delepierre's *Dissertation* (1861) on Antonio Rocco's *Alcibiade fanciullo a scola* (Venice, not as Mr Kearney records 'Oranges', 1652); and it is strange that the BL rejected these desiderata–if, that is, they ever reached it. Dr E. J. Dingwall, an official of the Museum and honorary keeper of the Private Case, was another of its generous benefactors, even managing to wrest a book from the library of the Revd A. R. T. Winkley (Kearney 1159). Winkley's penchant for goosing schoolboys bent over a comic (or perhaps a copy of *Rupert and the Black Dwarf*) at railway bookstalls landed him in trouble more than once. Leonard Green, a writer, not a pornographer, admitted indeed immediately to the *paradis* of the General Catalogue despite his two rather provocative titles, *Dream Comrades* and *The Youthful Lover,* which a less liberated 'placer' might have cast into the *enfer* of the Private Case, nearly found himself on a perjury charge when giving evidence of Winkley's good character during one of the clergyman's unfortunate mishaps. Winkley was a friend of Arthur Kenneth Searight (the man who introduced E. M. Forster to India). Searight was the author of six fat manuscript volumes of erotica which he circulated among his friends, five of which were unfortunately destroyed in a moment of panic by an urbane and cultured reprobate resident in Edinburgh; but the sixth, housed in a handsome blue half-morocco box by Bayntun (Dawes's regular book-binder, incidentally, although he did not always care to sign his work), happily survives in an excellent private collection in Hampshire. My reason for this seeming digression is to wonder whether the BL has a Private Case in its department of manuscripts also. Erotic manuscripts used to circulate freely in some circles. Indeed, the gentleman who consigned Searight to the flames lent me two manuscripts of his own, 'The Lost Lavatories of London' and 'Stimulating Letters', subjects on which the printed books in the Private Case remain silent. Perhaps Mr Kearney will touch on this matter when he issues his companion-volume of BL books once in PC but now de-suppressed. Further bequests, of more modern material, by Mr Beecher Moore, an American resident in London, and another American citizen, Mr J. B. Rund, including a volume bearing the happy title *Myra Learns the Ropes,* have ensured that the PC's holdings are wide-ranging and up-to-date.

It is to be hoped that Mr Legman's introduction will be printed separately. 'I have been writing in my peculiarly provocative way for nearly fifty years now,' he blandly asserts in this long and rumbustious essay, and nowhere has he been more peculiar or more provocative. In this instance he has it in for the late Pascal Pia, author of the standard French bibliography of erotica, *Les Livres de l'enfer,* and for Guillaume Apollinaire, 'smooth intellectual fake and *rastaquouère,*' whom he hurls from the pinnacle of fame usually accorded him of being the prime mover in the compilation of the erotica catalogue of the Bibliothèque Nationale, and exposes as a shameless plagiarist and cannabalizer. Especially interesting is Mr Legman's account of the history of the bespoke erotica written by Anaïs Nin and her circle for an American oil-millionaire. Miss Nin's productions are the type of book, together with those of Pierre Louÿs, of which Mr Legman thoroughly approves. He reserves his detestation for homosexuality and sadistic literature. It is a fascinating exercise, the jewel of which comes at the end of his paragraphs reiterating his theory that H. S. Ashbee is the author of *My Secret Life.* Be that as it may, there can be no better vignette for a Victorian 'subject' painting than the one he gives of Ashbee's wife discovering the distasteful truth and falling to the library floor with one of the fat little volumes in her hand, crying out like Margarete in the last scene of *Faust,* 'Henry! Henry!'

There is little to find fault with in this book except to lament the lack of indexes for publishers and titles donated by the PC's main benefactors and to say that a cure must be found for Mr Kearney's parenthesis-bacillus. Square brackets are the correct bibliographical symbols to enclose editorial information and, in any case, would be more typographically pleasing. It was Tom Lehrer, in an introduction to one of his songs, who admitted that 'dirty books are fun', and Mr Kearney's researches have clearly given him a good deal of amusement, as some of his comments show. Remarks such as 'this rather unstimulating performance' and 'Both magazines have dedications, one of which is rather rude' are in strong contrast to his predecessors in the field whose glosses always make them appear rather sobersides. I hear that some officials at BL are a little apprehensive of this book's appearance, fearing an influx of the dirty raincoat brigade. I do not know about a brigade, but my raincoat, of appalling squalor, is out, ready for the morning.

8
Epilogue

Hey bar-keep, what's keeping you?
Keep pouring drinks
For all these palookas
Hey, you know what I thinks.

Tom Waits

THIS eminently skippable epilogue came about only because the book wasn't long enough and after a casual request from my original publisher for another article, couched in the sort of peremptory amiability of a man adding an item to his weekly grocery order, had laid open the embarrassing truth that I did not know any more about the occult than what has gone before. I think it was Crowley who pointed out that common is to either sex (like *artifex* and *opifex*) the temptation to have a go at writing some sort of an autobiography. Antiquarian booksellers are bewilderingly susceptible to this discourageable vice, perhaps because of handling so many books by so many other people, unburdening themselves of things called *On My Shelves* and *My Silent Friends,* so I feel a need to stress editorial pressures and shallowness of knowledge before launching into self-indulgence to try and come at how I got into this game in the first place.

We were not an especially 'spooky' family. My great-aunt Zookie, short for what, I wonder?–was much given to Tarot readings, her cards, at least in daylight hours, tied permanently around her waist in a silken purse. Quick on the draw, for the most part, to benefit all comers with a 'reading', she, one day, felt inexplicably unwilling to put out the cards; after eventual persuasion she saw in them precisely nothing. Later that day the enquirer was despatched by a passing motor-car. My aunt, Pamela Frankau, has a pen-portrait of Zookie in her novel *Slaves of the Lamp,* second-sight being a continuing thread in the trilogy it makes up, and knowing my interest in magic asked me the procedure for tarot consultations. I recommended the quite complicated method of MacGregor Mathers, for whom I have great admiration, against the simpler layout of A. E. Waite; she mastered it splendidly and it is among the best chapters of the book. Pamela saw ghosts quite a lot; on one occasion smelled one. She and a friend had rented a villa in the south of France from the American hostess Elsa Maxwell. Set in the hills above Cannes it had, I recall, a certain gloomy charm. Pamela's stay was upset by a nightly visitation of a pair of clasped, white, female, beringed hands and an effluvium similar to drains in the last stages of dilapidation. Fearful of spoiling the holiday by speaking out, yet equally fearful of the manifestation itself, she sat up each night until dawn drinking brandy and trying to write. One day, fairly far on in the holiday, as they sat in a café, her companion took her by the shoulder and stared at her straight between the eyes. 'I can take the hands, Pamela,' she said, 'but I wish she didn't *smell*.'

Despite forty years of dabbling in occult waters, I have had only one 'experience', which I'll come to in a moment, but was a passive, indeed unknowing, agent in a second, its otherwise trite details remarkable for the sort of shared encounter (i.e. two people experiencing the same thing at the same time) that is so intriguing about Pamela's malodorous spectre. I was dining with the secretary of a peer of the realm whose hobby it was (maybe still is) to paint pictures of nude ladies: when models were unavailable to read literature in which that sex in similar disattire was a more or less recurrent theme. Once, with some difficulty, I acquired for him the two-volume American edition of *My Secret Life,* a Victorian autobiographical work very much along those lines and running to some 2400 pages, but it was returned by his secretary with the explanation that His Lordship found it too heavy to hold in bed. At home, my flat-mate was entertaining someone who would have more than graced, if he could have kept a grip on brush and palette, his Lordship's easel. His secretary's food tended towards the ethnic more than the appetizing; healthful, perhaps to be accounted 'cranky', fare from the more subservient states behind the Iron Curtain was her speciality. Probably thoughts touched on being back home again. I was looking forward to a finger or two of whisky, to hearing the new Rolling Stones album (*Aftermath* it must have been with the quite lovely, twelve-minute Jagger-Richards track 'Going Home', its yearnings not unakin to my own), perhaps the chance of what the Americans, with some justification, call 'Sloppy Seconds'. At any rate, some part of me could not wait, excused itself from the table–I recall a plethora of red cabbage, wine in quite astonishingly disproportionate quantities, red too, of the screw-top, supermarket class–and directed itself to where it and the rest of me, lived. Perhaps it was my 'aura'. I cannot say. Whatever it was that made off, its behaviour on arrival was unexemplary. My flat-mate and his girl were in the early, none the less for that essentially private, stages of the part of the evening's plans that had called for my absence. Both of them together–and that is what is interesting–heard from the corner of the room the sound of my voice. It spoke, they reported, in disguised but perfectly recognizable tones. 'Hello, hello', it intoned, rather like a policeman to offending motorists, 'What's going on here?' They sprang, as might be expected, apart, thoroughly alarmed. Michael telephoned my hostess and here is another odd thing. As she went to answer the call, she remarked, 'That will be for you.'

When I was seven someone gave me a conjuring set, a 'cabinet of magic' I expect the lid announced, after which as The Prince Kasan, 'a trick, a smile and a song,' I bored rigid an impressed and financially depleted audience with lengthy exhibitions of wonder-working and it may be that, finally disillusioned with the cups and balls, water into wine, the multiplying lighted candles (rather a show-stopper, that one), I began to instigate enquires into more rarefied areas of, as Crowley puts it, 'causing change to occur in conformity with Will.' At any rate, inspired by Dennis Wheatley's *Haunting of Toby Jugg,* a friend of mine and I were soon sacrificing spiders on a stone altar overhung with an inverted crucifix to the accompaniment of ungrammatical Latin prayers–read backwards or forwards, memory does not serve. Wheatley was not proscribed at home, perhaps because he was friendly with my grandfather, himself a novelist of some repute. Indeed he carried rather a torch for Wheatley since the two of them had bankrupted themselves in business and carved out new and successful careers as writers, going so far as to resign from the Royal Society of Literature when Wheatley's application for fellowship was turned down.

This sort of behaviour was allowed to plough on unchecked through public school whose library, by and large of the 'sound' variety (*Elephant Bill, The Crowthers of Bankdam,* that sort of thing), yielded a copy of Wilde's *Picture of Dorian Gray.* A reprehensible willowiness now topped occult posturings, encouraged much by traditional public-school atmosphere that nurtures that rather 'hothouse' mentality as zealously as it stamps out its physical manifestations.

> I think of all the jolly ways
> To please the endoderm.
> I'm hetero in the holidays
> And homo in the term.

That was much our motto. There is a good deal to be said for public-school behaviour of that kind, now I'm told rather on the decline, in that it is excellent practice, both mental and physical, for what, despite earnest campaigning by those who have never made it into other spheres, must still be considered the Real Thing.

At about that time the first edition of John Symonds's life of Aleister

Crowley, *The Great Beast*, came out. Up to then I had been rather keen on spiritualism, the bingo of the occult world as opposed to magic's roulette, if one may look on the subject, as I then did, as rather a game, although I'd recently become rather disillusioned with the cult, following a visit with my aunt to an exhibition of clairvoyance at the Wigmore Hall by Ronald Strong. Pamela, not all that keen on 'copy' (she once remarked to my cousin Ernest Raymond, about a novel of his that was perhaps too closely observed, 'Ernest, dear, your research is showing'), nonetheless required to set a scene where that sort of silliness was going on; and I happily accompanied her.

Strong–from flutterings, too much silk handkerchief, a great curtain of blonde, perhaps bleached, hair which he kept sweeping back with lily hands–seemed to have been carried rather further along the road of male-to-male affections than any of us at school reached even at our most languorous. He was 'controlled' by a member of the great battery of Red Indians–one imagines some enormous squawking empyreal chicken-run–from which spiritualists draw their guides, Red Eagle, White Owl, Grey Feather, some such name, whose descent was marked by violent tremors and to whom he spoke with the utmost condescension as if addressing a tiresome and not very bright lover. 'Yes, dear, I'll tell her,' 'Yes, dear, I'm *listening*,' he said as he fussed about the stage making contact with members of the audience for whom he had a 'message'. He was attended–backed up when inspiration failed, as it did from time to time–by two other persons on stage, a man and a woman. The former–in orders, a thin neck protruding from a clerical collar the pivot for a scraggy head that abetted farmyard comparisons already formed for the non-physical being in charge, more or less, of proceedings–raked the audience for signs of disaffection, and lowered itself now and again in a mumbled prayer. The woman was seated at a pianoforte. Her plump, dimpled, vastly jolly face, a certain over-application (considering the time of day) of mascara, a frock more shrilly patterned than perhaps Ronald Strong could have wished for, gave one to suspect, indeed irreverently to hope, that she might come out with something a little more boogified than the hymns she had been requested, most likely hired, to perform. She, like Strong, breathed a latent–in her case mainstream–sensuality, an oncomingness that proposed in other circumstances she would be willing to take on each of the male members of the congregation in turn, if time were found to be pressing two at once.

In a dreadful way Ronald Strong's performance was extremely impressive. He seemed, once he had established to whom he wished to speak, to home in on that person's private life, private grief for the most part, in a thoroughly disquieting ·and uncanny way. The messages he had for the bereaved were, however, of the tritest kind. Here Ronald Strong's imagination, un-uplifted by either the clergyman's prayers or an occasional rather barrelhouse interpretation of 'Approach, my soul, the mercy seat,' led him instead into shocking depths of banality of the 'vale of flowers' variety where he would have us believe all the departed, cheek by jowl, made their repose.

I came to see there was something quite undeniably seedy about spiritualism, or was in those days, as if the mediums, their guides, the whole ranks of the dear departed, were, like the British, in the grip of the same post-war austerity, cowed, dowdy, down-at-heel. Magic offered far more exotic possibilities.

There was trouble over *The Great Beast*. The bookseller from whom I had ordered it reported the fact to my housemaster, and I was hauled over the coals. It was not the first time I had brushed with censorship. The headmaster at my prep school had descended, after a tip-off, upon my tuck-box and discovered among the yo-yos and batting gloves four or five issues of an American monthly magazine called *Weird Tales*. Though they were not picture-strips, the 'horror comics' about which Britain at that time was stricken with a phobia of clinical proportions (I recall in a book underlining their dangers, the reproduction of a frame from one of them showing a New York cop discovering a woman's body and passing the thoroughly unnecessary observation, 'Gee, a dame, and she's been croaked') their coloured covers were on the alarming side. It was not long after my 'bust', as it were, that the publisher Victor Gollancz began issuing the stories of H. P. Lovecraft, a regular contributor to *Weird Tales*, between hard covers. I felt somehow vindicated, despite my aunt's dislike of Victor Gollancz–for reasons I've forgotten, perhaps irrational ones, for Pamela could love and hate with quixotic panache. The novelist, Elizabeth Bowen, was a pet aversion and she spent many hours making up scurrilous rhymes about this, it seems to me, quite excellent novelist. One such began:

Elizabeth Bowen,
Her petticoat showin',
Her forehead perspirin',
Was rapidly tirin'.
She was writin' a story so tender and passionate
She scarce had the strength left to put one more dash in it.
So hot were the words that her hero had spoken
That, twice, since the morning, her brassiere had broken.

I was sitting in the Ivy restaurant with Pamela one evening when Victor Gollancz came in. He stood looking about him in the middle of the room, light from a chandelier glowing on his bald, substantial, in its way not undistinguished head. 'That,' Pamela said, 'is Victor Gollancz. And that (she pointed upwards) is a chandelier. Do you suppose, with any luck...?'

It was Pamela who got me my first job, at Foyle's bookshop, her acquaintanceship with Christina Foyle easing the preliminaries. I do not

suppose she recited to Christina another of her poems:
Poor little Christina Foyle,
She never quite comes to the boil.
She froths and she bubbles, she hisses and steams
But the kettle-lid only comes off in her dreams.

I was posted to the theology department where, owing to the religious persuasions of the other staff, I was put in charge of the occult section. We were, in 1954, in the wake of Billy Graham's successful London evangelical crusade and several members of staff had been converted, religious fervour, so recently endowed, running rather high. I remember asking our under-manager how he had spent his weekend. His answer reduced me to a humble silence: 'I wrestled with My Lord in prayer.'

It was at Foyle's that I had my first love-affair, concomitant emotional stresses much eased by having read Proust, whose analyses of love-affairs, however, lengthy as they are, do not mention so far as I know how quite extraordinarily physically well being in love makes one feel. I never felt better in my life, despite Sylvia and my keeping some rather odd hours. It was the era of the coffee-bar—Bunjie's folk-cellar (round the corner from the Ivy) and the Gyre and Gimble by Charing Cross station being our favourite haunts. They were peopled by curious characters: Iron Foot Jack, one leg thus appended, who wore monogrammed, if grubby, silk shirts; and a devastatingly beautiful Ur-hippie called Cupid, son of a Polish diplomat. Cupid, on hard times, worked on a rubbish-tip feeding garbage into a furnace with a long spatula. Warmed by the flames and a fair quantity of some fierce red wine, Sylvia and I spent a pleasant evening watching him at his labours. Cupid's preferred beverage was concocted by crunching underfoot a plastic benzedrine inhaler and soaking the cotton-wool interior in a glass of water. Those were days before pills, the 'leapers' celebrated by The Who on their *Quadrophenia* album.

Love, though not of Sylvia, produced emotions, alarming in their onset, that were not categorized in *A la recherche du temps perdu*–feelings of insecurity, instability, even descending madness. Introspection on these threats to livelihood exacerbated the condition, whatever it was, to the point when in a mild way I began to get the 'horrors'. Those symptoms and a recurrence of them some years later coincided with periods when I was most deeply concerned with the occult and are the reason, most likely, I have never ventured very far along experimental lines. Doubtless they are manifestations of cowardice–unwillingness anyway to obey the four fundamental rules of magicianship: 'to know, to will, to dare, to keep silent.' At any rate, I decided to confine researches to the mundane, the bibliographical, side of the subject, sufficiently mentally stimulating but avoiding areas that had begun to make me uneasy.

I had always been intrigued by the physical phenomena of occultism. As a boy I had stared spellbound at the photograph of the brick suspended in mid-air in Harry Price's *End of Borley Rectory*, and, later, at the disgusting, purportedly ectoplasmic, exudations photographed by Baron Schrenk-Notzing for his *Phenomena of Materialization*. Just as I write this comes the news of the death of Eric John Dingwall, a member of the team who exposed Harry Price as rather a rogue. Dingwall, on decidedly more intelligent levels, shared my interest in the occult and in erotica (he was affectionately known as 'Dirty Ding' and did much to build up the British Library's holdings in that area). *The Times*'s obituarist very properly emphasized that it is for his researches into the paranormal he should be remembered, particularly in the area of nineteenth-century hypnotic phenomena; but for a spirited 'read' it is hard not to prefer his two books on the mechanical devices aimed at putting paid to the pleasures, indeed to the feasibility, of sexual intercourse, *The Girdle of Chastity* and *Male Infibulation*. The latter is a rare book. Published in 1925 and not proving to be a runaway best-seller, much of the stock remained in the publisher's warehouse, which became the target for one of the earlier and more ferocious bombing-raids by the Luftwaffe. Dingwall seems to have shared my aunt's quixoticism of love and hate, after the death of his second wife never recovering from the deep depression into which it had cast him and having got rid of his first by the simple expedient of losing her on the Underground.

Pamela, for lost people, objects too–those she wanted (unlike Dingwall and his first wife) to relocate–evoked the help of St Antony of Padua, for whom she had an especial devotion. He was often called upon for other purposes and almost always turned up trumps. She was possessed, well, we all were, by a relative, my grandfather's brother Ronald, a celebrated but pungent music-hall comedian and, far more reprehensible in my nanny's eyes, a paid-up member of the British Communist party, to whom politeness, family piety anyway, demanded an invitation should be extended for Pamela's wedding which took place during the same war that had been responsible for the destruction of the stock of *Male Infibulation*. Pamela dragged off her surprised fiancé to Westminster Cathedral in a taxi and prostrated herself before a statue of her favourite saint. 'Please, St Antony, let Uncle Ronnie be on tour in Birmingham,' she prayed. Shortly afterwards she received a letter from her uncle. It read, 'Dear Pamela: It is most kind of you to invite me to your wedding but, alas, that week I shall be on tour in Birmingham.' Pamela dropped the letter, grabbed her husband-to-be and hurtled (again by taxi) back to the Cathedral. There, having given thanks to her saint, she ended by saying, 'Oh, by the way, I should have explained. It didn't have to be Birmingham, it could have been Liverpool.'

Our table at Bunjie's folk-cellar was sometimes joined by Michael Houghton, proprietor of the Atlantis Bookshop, and it was during a conversation there that Houghton promised to introduce me to the friend and disciple of Aleister Crowley, Fra. N.·. He had a flat in Montague Square where he showed me for the first time his Crowley treasures. His death last year saddened me terribly. Fra. N.·. was quite extraordinarily kind and helpful, as well as being the most convivial and straightforward occultist (ex-occultist, rather) I have ever known. Occultists I find are inclined to moroseness, even downright gloom, Gerard Heym (about whom later) perhaps its foremost exponent. But Fra. N.·. enjoyed life to the full. He shared my passion for cricket (he had kept wicket for Eton and once played first-class cricket for Gloucestershire and thus is ensured of a place, along with another unlikely first-class cricketer, Samuel Beckett, in the pages of the Association of Cricket Statisticians' *Who's Who of Cricketers*) and owned an enormous country house where he once entertained the Rolling Stones. After supper Mick Jagger asked if they might smoke. Fra. N.·. hospitably pushed the cigarette-box towards him, but it was not tobacco the band had in mind to consume. Fra. N.·. was asked if he would care to indulge. 'Good Lord, no' he said. 'When Old Crow sent me on a magical retirement to Tunisia I found on arrival I'd forgotten to pack my tobacco. Forced to smoke that beastly stuff for nearly a month.'

Fra. N.·. favoured a pipe. It was of recalcitrant ignition. One day in the 1960s when I was running the rare book department of The Times Bookshop, he came in to examine some manuscripts we had acquired by the crystal-gazer, Frederick Hockley. He settled in a corner. I got on with some work. Later on I looked over to find Fra. N.·. completely engulfed from head to foot in a cloud of smoke far heavier than his pipe, capacious though it was, could possibly be producing. To my horror a small tongue of flame could be discerned in the area, only then to be guessed at, of Fra. N.·.'s waistline. I battered my way through the smoke where, within its envelope, I found Fra. N.·. calmly extinguishing a blazing box of Swan Vestas into which he had tidily but carelessly replaced a spent but still red hot match. He was completely unconcerned, indeed expectant of some small disaster striking him down. 'Serves me right for reading magical manuscripts without taking, ah, certain precautions,' he remarked. 'When I was raising at university the spirit of Mars, some of the coals from the fire leaped out of the grate and set light to the carpet. One expects that sort of thing, of course. Shows one's working along the right lines.'

Another occultist who liked cricket was Charles Richard Cammell. In fact he died while watching on television a Test Match at the Oval, over-excitement at proceedings, judging by Wisden's reportage on the game, not be be adjudged the primary cause of demise. His wife told me his last words had been 'It is finished'. It says little for my grasp of history that it was only considerably later that it dawned on me the line was unoriginal. Somebody ought to do a dictionary of last words. Crowley's 'I am perplexed' seems to be apocryphal, perhaps also King George V's 'Bugger Bognor'. My grandfather's reflected his distaste for one of the branches of the arts: 'I do hope there won't be music.'

It is a shame Fra. N∴ did not write more about Crowley. He edited and revised Crowley's *777* for Michael Houghton, wrote a couple of introductions to books on the occult, and contributed a fine obituary of Crowley to the *Occult Observer,* another Houghton publication. Houghton, in size and personality, was the very opposite of Fra. N∴, almost a dwarf, his demeanour exactly comparable with that of Grumpy in *Snow White and the Seven Dwarfs.* There had been some 'bother' in the past, I heard, that had made the newspapers, attentions rather forced upon a lady who–accounts differing–either found him objectionable, or, encouraged at first by a not unflattering courtship, had discovered masculine appurtenances to be disappointingly commensurate with overall stature. At any rate, Houghton had made some midnight and unauthorized foray into her bedroom where she had managed to fight him off and, after he had made his escape, to ring the police. In defence, Houghton explained that he had indeed visited the lady's bedroom, but not in his physical body. She had been a witness to a remarkable, perhaps also a daring, exhibition of astral projection. The court was inclined to disagree.

I had for a long time thought of mounting an exhibition of rare books on the occult but it was not until 1965 that I could persuade The Times Bookshop to put it on. Unknown to its directors the shop had become quite well known to collectors of the arcane, not to say the improper, and the astute collector could always find among the Arthur Rackhams and bound sets of Surtees some rather disreputable nugget such as Swinburne's *Whippingham Papers,* one of the more salacious novels referred to in Mario Praz's *Romantic Agony,* or a copy of Pierre Louÿs' *Manuel de civilité pour les petites filles à l'usage des maisons d'éducation,* quite my favourite book of that genre. I was lucky to get away with it, I suppose. In those days before The Times's absolute decline, certain standards had to be kept up (woe betide anyone who failed to capitalize the 'T' of The, for instance) and previous exhibitions had been on the stodgy side. 'Witchcraft', as the catalogue was called, was at last seen as a likely crowd-drawer. The newspaper was initiating a series of advertisements with the slogan, 'Top People Take The Times,' which we in Wigmore Street regarded as an uncommendable *snobisme* and countered with a campaign reading 'Not Only Top People Go to The Times Bookshop.' Classes below that which the board considered 'top' were not thought to be book-buyers. Indeed, The Times's chairman, John Walter, whose wife owned the crossest face of any woman I have ever seen (at the opening of the John Masefield exhibition I feared she might pull a gun and turn it on the crowd rather after the manner of Sid Vicious in the video of 'My Way') was asked at a board meeting if we might paint our name on the shop blinds so that passengers on the tops of buses would know a bookshop lay beneath them. 'I wasn't aware', was his reply, 'any of our customers travelled by bus.'

All the books at the exhibition were for sale (we sold every English book printed before 1700 on the first morning) at prices that now seem absurdly low. Ludovic Lavater's *De spectris* (Geneva, 1570) cost fifteen pounds, the first edition of Jean Bodin's *De la démonomanie des sorciers* (Paris, 1580) was a hundred, a fine copy of M. R. James's *Ghost-Stories of an Antiquary* (1904) seems even then a bargain at four pounds. It was especially pleasing to be able to offer an alchemical book, Franciscus Kieser's *Cabala Chymica* (Mühlhausen, 1606) that had belonged to Mary Anne Atwood and her father, Thomas South. This we had acquired from Gerard Heym, a curious character if ever one walked the earth.

Heym was a practising alchemist, or so he put it about. Certainly he contributed articles to the alchemical quarterly *Ambix*. In earlier days he was reputed to have been rich, the possessor of a fine library of Tibetan manu-scripts and early spagyrical books 'of the last rarity', as Montague Summers would have put it. When I knew him, towards the end of his life, he had fallen on hard times, the pearl of great price conspicuously, sometimes embarrass-ingly elusive. To cover shortage of money, he spoke enigmatically of a Trust, its executors uncommunicative, unavailable by telephone, unreceptive to postal requests, perhaps (so extremely distant did he make them sound) of non-tellurian origins. This may have been a stratagem to disguise financial problems that were nothing more than the run-of-the-mill shortages everyone suffers from now and again, derivation of funds deliberately obfuscated to promote an air of mystery. For Heym was mysterious about absolutely everything, calculatedly, provocatively mysterious, cloaking the very sim-plest of news in mists of A. E. Waitian impenetrability. Dark clouds were gathering; the Masters foresaw a bleak future; magic, and that of a pretty perverted variety, was abroad, a canker in the land. His words were projected in no more than a whisper from a plump, battered, bullet-headed, blue-eyed face that gave him the look of a minor, though not at all to be unreckoned-with, henchman in the Third Reich. Indeed it was rumoured that Heym had once been photographed with Hitler riding in an open limousine. Where he came from I never found out. Origins, like everything else, were designedly obscured. Business transactions, however, provided they were of a cash-in-hand nature, were remarkably simply executed, settled over tea in a dark corner of the now defunct Devonshire Club abutting the Ritz, the Trustees, if they existed, settling for modest, occasionally derisory, sums for the books he had to offer. The money trousered, Heym was inclined slightly to brighten, enough anyway to expand, though no less imperspicuously, on sunnier occult horizons than earlier propounded. There was a continental lodge, operating from Paris, that was doing splendid work. I must make efforts to join them at the earliest opportunity. News had already been received of my utmost suitability for membership. Would I not make up my mind to go over soon? Had he ever mentioned he had once seen the Masters in a box at Covent Garden? Would I care to buy the correspondence of Mrs Atwood with Isabelle de Steiger. The Trustees...

In that case the Trustees' modest estimate of value was correct. It was a dreadfully dull series of letters, the scribbles of an old woman on the weather and her ailments. Shortly afterwards I heard that Heym had died; in obedience to alchemical tradition, he had destroyed all his papers.

The Beatles came to our witchcraft exhibition, all but Ringo, perhaps not to be accounted 'booky'. Their visit was proposed by Jane Asher, then Paul McCartney's girlfriend. We had done the valuation of her father's T. E. Lawrence collection and of Miss Asher's collection of Lewis Carroll first editions, and I think she must have advised McCartney to invest some of his new-found wealth in antiquarian books. Lennon was in abrasive mood, George Harrison silent, McCartney disarming, talkative, enthusiastic. Jane Asher's friendship with him had rather upset family life. Her father, a surgeon I think, high-up, anyway, in the medical world, grew thoroughly disturbed by all the publicity and took himself off on some protracted holiday which the press reported as a 'disappearance'. Mrs Asher, however, rather entered into the spirit of things, floating into the bookshop in a kaftan and saying things like 'wow' and 'man'. We had our fair share of hippies at the exhibition, a class that did not much appeal, although I would not go as far as Wild Willie Barrett's aspersions on the movement where he sings:

I hate bleeding hippies so I give them head-butts

a song promptly banned by the BBC as inciting violence. A movement that spawned the rock groups Love and, when it pulled itself together, the Grateful Dead, cannot be wholly bad. Many critics cite the Doors as the most influential band of the movement, but, despite their name being taken from Aldous Huxley's *Doors of Perception*, this seems altogether incorrect. There is arguably a certain rambling transcendentalism about the lyrics of Jim Morrison–an unpleasant character if ever there was one, his behaviour towards groupies, that thoroughly useful section of society, being especially deplorable–but they were never an 'acid' band any more than, say, Big

Brother and the Holding Company, who also jumped on the hippie band-wagon. Musically, Morrison had more feeling for black music than Janis Joplin, who sings like the white middle-class Texan girl she was so keen to expunge. (I'm not saying, like Pete Townshend, that whites can't sing 'black': listen, for instance, to Charlie Musselwhite.)

It was the hippies, though, who put paid to my Crowley bibliography, seizing on his books and reprinting them in all sorts of clandestine forms that resisted researches into their origins and their print runs.

When I left The Times Bookshop and went into partnership with Jean Overton Fuller, another musician was almost our first customer, Jimmy Page of Led Zeppelin. I am afraid I did not recognize him. I had not really been following the British rhythm-and-blues boom that led to the formation of the 'heavy' rock-groups of the late sixties, although Sylvia and I used to sit at the feet of Chris Barber's jazz-band in 100 Oxford Street, which had much to do with its popularization, and so was unfamiliar with the Yardbirds, in which Jimmy, like Jeff Beck and Eric Clapton before him, had flowered into one of Britain's greatest rock guitarists. His visit coincided with a period when the corridor outside our office was being redecorated, the painters' transistor radio interrupting, indeed drowning, conversation. Rather petulantly I kicked the door shut and remarked to Jimmy that I could not stand pop music. He politely said nothing and it was not until he handed me his cheque with his name printed on it that I realized who he was.

Once I established that Zeppelin was firmly, if distortedly, rooted in the blues tradition I came to like their music very much. One only has to listen to the quite chilling 'In My Time of Dying', where Jimmy reiterates a guitar riff first acoustically performed by the Texan singer Blind Willie Johnson in 1927 and where Robert Plant sounds as if he is being dragged screaming skywards in the claws of some not quite wholly benign archangel, to understand how sensitively, if loudly, Zeppelin pays homage to its roots. Jimmy's interest in Crowley has resulted in poor treatment by the press, now and again the sort of thing Crowley himself had to put up with, despite their being practically no reference to the occult in their lyrics. Aural evidence has not, however, satisfied Pastor Jacob Aranza of Louisiana who has delivered himself of a booklet entitled *Backward Masking Unmasked: Backward Satanic Messages of Rock and Roll Exposed*, wherein he states that Led Zeppelin's 'Stairway to Heaven' if played backwards (on what sort of machine, one wonders) yields the line, 'There's no escaping it. It's my sweet Satan.' There is not much escaping either the good pastor's preternaturally low credulity ceiling nor, it must be said, his industry in producing his guide in the teeth of a punishing schedule of burning rock-and-roll records in public places aided by his youthful converts.

In its day jazz was considered on the improper side. It certainly was at my prep school towards the end of the forties, which was perhaps my reason for taking to it so pleasurably. We were an intensely unmusical family, evidenced by my grandfather's dying words. His mother took things a stage further. Visiting a music-hall where, from the front of the circle, a marksman with a repeater rifle picked out a tune by firing at the keys of a grand piano on stage below, she remarked it was a pity the pianist was not sitting at the keyboard. As ill luck would have it the nearest prep-school to where we lived was St George's, Windsor Castle. All but twenty of us were choristers in the royal chapel and our duty was to attend the lengthy sung Matins and Evensong every Sunday. I was totally unprepared for the very considerable shock of Good Music. In those days, the order of service was printed on a folio sheet of paper placed in every pew so it could be worked out, sermon apart, or so I thought, how long we could expect to be cornered. The anthem on my first morning seemed marvellously short, some such words as 'Moab is my wash-pot, Amen' appearing on the service-sheet. I was appalled, therefore, when the choir, having sung them lustily out, began them all over again. They were not, after all, printed twice. Nor was that the end of it. To every conceivable harmony, disharmony to my ears, the words were tossed ceaselessly from Decani to Cantoris and back again so that the thing spun itself out over a quarter of an hour or more. It seemed monstrously unfair. That was the end of Good Music for me. Apart from one master who played passable boogie-woogie piano under threat of dismissal, nothing decent came to my ears until my last term. A non-singing colleague of mine who had told me my first rude joke (Bus-conductor: 'Now, jump up ma'am, and show your agility.' Woman: ' Oh, you rude man, of course I shan't') slunk into the library, a twelve-inch 78 under his blazer. He dragged the rugger socks out of the gramophone (they damped down volume), changed the soft needle for a loud one, cranked it up and switched on. Louis Armstrong's cornet leaped from the machine like sparks struck from a great golden anvil. It was 'Back o'Town Blues.' The gravelly, quite lovely voice, which cocked the biggest possible snook at the choristers who had gathered around and stared at the two of us as if we were locked in an unnatural embrace, began to unload in the library the thick, tarry burden of the song:

I had a woman living way back o'town.
She treated me right, never would let me down.
But I wasn't satisfied, I had to run around.

In leaped Jack Teagarden's trombone trailing its dirty purple robes in the dust behind it. I was hooked. A lot of people cannot listen to Armstrong after the Hot Five and Seven recordings of 1926-8. For a while I became just such a purist, refusing to listen to any jazz that featured the saxophone, a quite unjustifiable snobbishness. In late middle-age I enjoy the saxophone, especially in rhythm-and-blues. A good rhythm-and-blues saxophonist should give the impression not only that he is picking his nose but is smearing the findings along a highly polished and expensive surface.

I became rather a purist in magical matters as well, the Golden Dawn seeming to me to have got things mostly right. Quite what spark within me, and by whom implanted, was touched off, I do not know. Despite their reputation for scarcity, three out of the four volumes of Regardie's text were readily available until about 1970 by the simple expedient of ordering them from the Chicago publishers, so I had a certain grounding when I joined up.

The practical drawback of the Golden Dawn system is that it is very expensive to get going. Like cricket, it needs a lot of people, a lot of equipment and considerable space (reasons, among others, why Crowley switched to sex-magic). In his last years Regardie compiled a method of self-initiation (printed in his recension of the Golden Dawn material which displays some curious additions and even more curious deletions), a bed-sit approach, as it were, but there is an ignobility about it somehow. Of course a lot of people means a lot of trouble, ostensibly the cause of the Order's demise, but the real problem was most likely a psychic one. The psychic pitfall of the Golden Dawn lay in the practice of the assumption of god-forms. There are ways of doing this, step by step, with reference to the Tetragrammaton from Heh final to Yod in that order, but even then it is a fairly dangerous game unless precautions are taken. There is not much point in safely ascending a high building by using the staircase if, to come down again, you are going to do so by throwing yourself off the roof.

Round about the time I mounted the witchcraft exhibition I belonged to an occult group working along Golden Dawn lines. It was there that I had my only 'experience', mild though it was. The Order's chief was a charming lady for whom I had the highest respect. She spoke fluent Enochian but needed watching when manipulating her magic sword for fear, in the small Hampstead flat where ceremonies took place, she should pin one to the wall. We had been meditating on the sphere of Yesod on the Tree of Life and I fear I was growing fidgety. It had been some time since my last cigarette and there was the promise, as always after meetings, of a delicious, if vegetarian, supper. Baked potatoes, what the Americans (and our leader hailed from New York) call Idaho potatoes, were her *forte*. Attention was drawn back into proceedings by the awareness that each member was being asked in turn if, in the course of the ritual, he or she had 'seen' anything. I'm afraid I had not. Thoughts throughout had been of the earthiest. It came to me that it would be necessary to invent some sort of received vision, nothing too far-fetched for fear that would call for elaboration, delaying supper as well, for that matter. I decided to say that I had found myself standing on castle ramparts, below me a silver flowing river, its ox-bow–rather good, that–encircling a high artificial mound on which the castle (a medieval one it could be added, giving at least some idea of time-travelling) had been raised. I bided my time, contemplation returning to the Idaho potatoes. At last my neighbour's turn came round. I would be next. 'What did you see, Frater —, in the sphere of Yesod,' enquired our leader. 'I had the distinct impression,' my neighbour replied, 'of standing on castle ramparts. Below me a silver river encircled the high mound of land on which the castle had been erected.' It was, he maddeningly added, of medieval construction.

This sort of mind-reading, though who was reading whose was never discovered, is probably quite common. Other magical phenomena within the group I began to find hard to accept. Magic works if you believe it does, and as I progressed in the order I found myself going slightly out of kilter. I feared a return of morbid thoughts of madness and violence. Abruptly–and I am afraid, also rudely–I resigned.

Probably I should long ago also have kicked my curiosity with erotica. There was something about the decidedly 'churchy' atmosphere of my prep-school, nestling at the foot of a medieval castle (and the likely source, now I come to think of it, for my contrived Yesodic 'vision'), experienced in tandem with some flattering wooing by pedophiles from whose ranks the staff seemed exclusively drawn, that prepared me for the equally cloying and clandestine world of the erotic–perhaps more fairly, dirty–book. In those days availability in this country of risky material was confined to books on practical matters, one in particular, *The Red Light* by Rennie McAndrew, because of a saturation-aimed advertising campaign and the fact that it was despatched from the publisher 'under plain wrapper', gaining it a pretty wide circulation. Doctor McAndrew became more expansive with his learning (*The Red Light* was disappointingly short perhaps for postal purposes) in a fat, almost a 'bumper', encyclopedia alphabetically arranged if memory serves; but there was a tameness about his findings, a childlike innocence, almost, radiating from his pages that was deeply unsatisfying. Luckily appetite could be sated, in time impaired, by a selection of equally stout volumes that treated of psychological as well as biological goings-on. The latter had been more or less mastered, thanks to a talk intriguingly illustrated with lantern-slides delivered to new boys at public school. It was prefaced by a mumbled word of introduction from the head before he slid embarrassed from the room. 'Well, boys,' he said, 'I expect you all know how a motor-car works, how an aeroplane works. But do you know how you work?' He introduced our informant. His name was Doctor Matthews. He made, so I heard, quite a reasonable living travelling about talking to adolescent boys to whom, in fact, he gave much comfort, for, despite being a psychiatrist (and a pioneer experimenter with LSD) he was of practical bent. His message, veiled though it was, even 'backwardly masked' in the manner of the satanic sentences on rock-and-roll records, came over loud and clear. Nobody ever came to any harm from a good screw. He might not have been quite so confident about our indulging in some of the 'problems' encountered by the authors of those consulting-room textbooks which now engaged my attention.

They were all of a pattern. An introductory chapter on the history and causes of the particular oddness was then supplemented with 'case histories', to prove, presumably, that the author was not making the whole thing up. Habits of patients (if they existed) were formed early, usually at the hands of nursemaids, and proved hard to break; sometimes they engaged the attention of the authorities. There was one extra-recalcitrant character, I remember, who, arrested in a public place in the act of his particular, somewhat gymnastic, misdemeanour and hurled into a prison-van, performed, to some applause, the same act on everyone else who happened to be inside. I forget from which book that incident came. They were all much of a muchness: Krafft-Ebing's *Psychopathia Sexualis,* Havelock Ellis's *Studies in the Psychology of Sex,* Magnus Hirschfeld's *Anomalies and Perversions,* Dr Stekel's *Patterns of Psycho-Sexual Infantilism,* George Henry's *Sex Variants,* Frank Caprio's *Variations of Sexual Behaviour.*

It is a great pity not more of Hirschfeld has appeared in English. Nothing escaped his net, from algolagnia to zoophilia, his findings set down in five enormous German volumes, *Geschlechtskunde, auf Grund dreissigjährigen Forschung und Erfahrung bearbeitet.* Many sets were destroyed by the Nazis, from which the English digest, reputedly translated by Arthur Koestler when in financially low waters, was culled. There exists a cartoon of Hirschfeld (affectionately nicknamed Auntie Magnesia) in top hat, frock-coat, spongebag trousers and a rolled umbrella, ascending a monumental column at whose apex a distinguished soldier or politician is sculpted in stone. 'Why do you not have a woman up there with you?' Hirschfeld is saying. 'Is it perhaps because you are an Urning?'

I bought a presentation copy of Hirschfeld's autobiography (the German version, again far fuller than the English) from Gerald Hamilton, a friend of Crowley's and the original of Christopher Isherwood's 'Mr Norris.' Hamilton, then leading a sedentary life in Chelsea above a Chinese restaurant called the Good Earth ('better to live above the good earth than beneath it,' he observed), had had a long innings as a confidence trickster of some efficiency, his favourite dodge being played on deposed European monarchs, to whom he claimed he had an *entrée* into British royal circles that could bring his victim back into favour—indeed, if the money were right, onto the throne. (There may have been some truth in this. He wrote to me once, 'I have had such a charming letter from the Duke of Windsor. It is marked "Private and Confidential" so I will show it to you when you come.') He was once shooting this line with one of those ousted crowned heads who happened to be travelling incognito with his French mistress. She appeared at breakfast one morning in poor temper, rubbing the back of her neck as if she had cricked it or damaged a vertebrae. 'Vous avez mal au cou, Madame?' Gerald politely began. She settled to her coffee and shot Gerald a look of considerable fury: 'Si vous devriez faire ce que je dois faire avec Son Altesse, vous auriez aussi le mal au cou.'

The case histories began to pall, tedium coinciding with a holiday in the south of France where for the first time I read, and indeed bought with my own money and speaking in French, my first pornographic novel. Some sort of literary taste must have formed in a ghastly way, comparable to the sort of mould on a culture that, unpleasant as it looks, turns out (like penicillin) to have beneficial qualities. It was John Cleland's *Memoirs of a Woman of Pleasure* (*Fanny Hill*, as it is better known). Literary stylishness is displayed in equal proportions to the art, as A. P. Herbert described it, 'of making the reader as randy as possible as often as possible.' Certainly it did that, though my chosen site for its perusal, Nice's acutely pebbly and much populated beach, was unwisdom on a grand scale. Discomfort, embarrassment, soon nothing short of physical agony cut distressingly across Cleland's joyous pages. There was the question too of where it should be hidden in readiness for the return car journey with my mother and my aunt, a problem with which Constant Lambert, more heavily clad, was also faced with a book he had just purchased on the *quais* in Paris and wished to conceal from Lytton Strachey who had suddenly put in an appearance. Lambert's purchase–Anthony Powell tells the story–was *Slavey* by 'Captain Teach'. I see now how rather disgraceful expertise, if it can be put so loftily, in this sort of material can be. Life, though, has somehow got to be lived, its bumpy courses, not dissimilar to the seafront at Nice, to be negotiated as painlessly as possible. John Fogerty, founder of my favourite rock band, Creedence Clearwater Revival, has perhaps given the answer on his album *Centerfield*. His fierce, angry, exuberant voice cuts disarmingly across those moments of regret for time ill-spent:

Sometimes I think
Life is just a rodeo
The trick is to ride
And make it to the bell.
Looks as if I might.

1 John Symonds and Kenneth Grant (eds), *The Magical Record of the Beast 666: the Diaries of Aleister Crowley 1914-1920* (London, Duckworth, 1972).

2 Some were published under the pseudonym of Edward Kelly in *The International: A Review of Two Worlds,* an American journal to which Crowley prolifically contributed during the First World War. Collected in book-form as *The Scrutinies of Simon Iff,* edited with an Introduction by Martin Starr (Chicago, Teitan Press, 1987).

3 *The Gospel According to St Bernard Shaw,* not published in his lifetime but not, as John Symonds and Kenneth Grant state in their edition of Crowley's *Magick* (London, Routledge and Kegan Paul, 1973), p 323, still unpublished. An edition, reproduced from typescript, was published by the Thelema Publishing Company, Barstow, California, pp [iv], 238, in 1953.

4 Stephen Skinner (ed), *The Magical Diaries of...Aleister Crowley...1923* (Jersey, Neville Spearman, 1979).

5 *Magick,* op. cit., p 131. Crowley's spelling is not only an archaism to 'distinguish the Science of the Magi from all its counterfeits' (*Magick* p 45): the six letter word balanced against the orthodox five is the balance of the hexagram and the pentagram. $6 + 5 = 11$, 'the general number of magick, or energy tending to change' (Crowley, *777: vel, prolegomena symbolica ad systemam sceptico-mysticae via explicandae, fundamentum hieroglypicum sanctissimorum scientiae summae,* London, Walter Scott, 1909, pxxv). 'K' is the eleventh letter in the alphabet. It is the initial letter of *kteis,* which, with *phallos,* is the most important weapon in Crowley's magical armoury. We shall be confronted with similar numerical correspondences in the course of this essay and it is the sort of problem with which Crowley's bibliographer will have to do battle.

6 The date is persistently and, as we shall see, erroneously given as 1929. Stephen Skinner, op. cit., p 13, more specifically states 12 April 1929; but this was the date Crowley received an advance copy from the printer (letter from Crowley to Fra N.·., Paris, 13 April 1929, Warburg Institute). The late Fra N.·. was briefly a disciple of Crowley, for the rest of his life a tireless collector of his books and manuscripts. For over twenty years he allowed me free access to all his papers and I would like to acknowledge my gratitude here for all his help and encouragement over that period. The Warburg Institute, London, now houses his collection.

7 Israel Regardie, *The Golden Dawn: an Account of the Teachings, Rites and Ceremonies,* 4 vols. (Chicago, Aries Press, 1937-1940), III, 152.

8 Regardie, IV, 51.

9 Regardie, II, 212-28.

10 Regardie, II, 25-8.

11 Officer in charge. There are occult significances about this personage, as there are about all the Officers in the ceremony. Document Z1, Regardie, III, 116-23, expounds upon them.

12 Herald, guardian, watcher: another Officer.

13 Representative of the goddess of Truth and Justice.

14 He represents Horus.

15 Regardie, III, 218-19.

16 *Sic.* The sun's position is correctly 18°52'45"Aries. This is one of many misprints that vermiculate Crowley's books. I am grateful to Miss Jean Overton Fuller for this and other

astrological information used herein.

17 Regardie, II, 245-63.

18 The capital 'I' represents 22. 22 + 18 = 40, i.e. the fortieth year after the reception of *The Book of the Law* in 1904.

19 Regardie, I, 191-202.

20 Regardie, IV, 51.

21 The black cloth binding is the first issue. It has been thought that the more elaborate and expensive white gold-blocked buckram binding took precedence but *The Equinox*, Vol. I, No. 6 (September 1911), [125], clearly states: 'the second edition [sic] is...bound in v/hite buckram, with colour design in gold.'

22 Actually the very first issue is in crimson paper wrappers with no statement of 'edition' on the title-page and consisted of only ten copies on paper and three on vellum. The other issues are all bound in blue wrappers.

23 Vellum as a binding, as opposed to a text-paper, is not a talismanic but a practical consideration and is dealt with in part II below.

24 Crowley's magical publications were each given a number, not a chronological one but one reflecting the content of the book itself. These are explained in *The Equinox*, Vol. I, No. 10 (September 1913), 41-56.

25 Like Crowley's *Collected Works* (Foyers, 1904-7) they are found in three volumes in white cloth, in black cloth, and in vellum; and bound as a single volume with similar variant binding materials. Again like the *Collected Works*, vellum-bound copies are supplied with green silk ties to prevent the vellum from warping; see part II below.

26 The name, pronounced Boll-éss-kinn, of Crowley's house on the shores of Loch Ness in the village of Foyers, Inverness-shire.

27 Crowley's motto ('I will endure') in the Outer Order of the Golden Dawn and his grade, or, rather, the one to which he considered he had attained in the Inner One, the Ordo Rosae Rubeae et Aureae Crucis.

28 Aleister Crowley, *The Confessions,* ed. John Symonds and Kenneth Grant (London, Cape, 1969), p 680.

29 University of Texas, Austin. There were two impressions of *Book Four Part One*, distinguishable by the publisher's address which in the first reads on pp.[ii] and [95] '3 Great James Street, Bedford Row' and in the second '33 Avenue Studios, South Kensington.' Some copies of the first impression carry a red paper slip announcing the change of address from W.C. to S.W. In a letter to Fra. N∴ [Paris] 8 February [1928], Crowley recollects: 'I think 500 of both part I and II at first. Then 1,500 or 2,000 more of Part I. Not sure if pt 2 was reprinted. Fancy war stopped it. Not sure.' Crowley is probably remembering correctly. Part Two is less commonly met with. Both impressions of Part One contain a misprint, 'practical' for 'tactical' on p. 47.

30 *Confessions,* loc. cit.

31 Fra. N∴'s transcript, Warburg Institute.

32 Crowley to Fra.N∴, 17 May [1928], Warburg Institute.

33 Crowley to Fra. N∴, Paris, 5 November 1928, Warburg.

34 Not one thousand as Symonds and Grant state in their edition of *Magick* (1973), p xv.

35 Charles Baudelaire, *Little Poems in Prose.* Translated by Aleister Crowley. With

Several Added Versions of the Epilogue by Various Hands and Twelve Copper Plate Engravings from the Original Drawings by Jean de Bosschère (Paris, Edward W Titus, 1928). This was a reissue of the sheets of the Wieland, London, edition of 1913 with an additional signature, L^8 (L3+1), and with the illustrations appearing for the first time.

36 Typescript, Warburg.

37 Crowley in a prospectus for the 'fourth' (though, as we shall see, it was the seventh) edition of *The Book of the Law,* London, 1937. He had already received oracular intimation of this conflict through the seer-ship of Victor Neuburg and Bartzabel, the spirit of Mars. See Francis King, *The Magical World of Aleister Crowley* (London, Weidenfeld and Nicolson, 1977), p. 62.

38 *Magick,* ed. Symonds and Grant, p 233.

39 The numerical equivalent of Al, the Hebrew word for God. Crowley also ascribed to it the number CCXX, 220 being the number of verses in the book and a synthesis of the ten sephiroth on the Tree of Life and their twenty-two connecting paths.

40 I.e. 1904.

41 *Sic*: see footnote 16.

42 Regardie, IV, 112-136. The Golden Dawn, however, in rare practical mood, compromised by the use of random pencil dashes on a sheet of paper.

43 [Paris, August or September 1928], Warburg.

44 If, as we probably must, we date the beginning of the Sino-Japanese war from the day of the 'incident' on the Marco Polo bridge outside Peking, 7 July 1937, Crowley's 'child' was about a fortnight overdue.

45 Turnbull & Spears set the preliminaries and pages 1-248 and 355-400a; Chiswick set pages 249-354 and 401-440.

46 Thenceforward, subsequent numbers were devoted to separate texts; Volume III, No. 4 (1939) was *Eight Lectures on Yoga*; III, 5 (1944) *The Book of Thoth*; III,6 posthumously but ritualistically issued at 6.19 a.m., the commencement of the autumnal equinox of 1961, by the Thelema Publishing Company at West Point, California, was *Liber Aleph, or, the Book of Wisdom and Folly. Liber Aleph* had been intended to be *The Equinox,* Vol. III, No. 5 and had been announced in Crowley's *Khing Kang King.* The war prevented its publication. Symonds and Grant (Crowley's *Magick,* op. cit., p. 6) can only suggest 'circa 1939' as the publication date of *Khing Kang King*, but in fact it is a solsticial one, clearly imprinted on p.2, 'An Ixiii Sol in 0^0 Cancer 7.40 a.m. June 22, 1939 e.v.'

47 Crowley to Fra N.·., London, 8 September [1936], Warburg.

48 Pearl Brookesmith to Fra. N.·., 25 September 1936, Warburg.

49 It did not, however, sell out. Copies, unpleasantly rebound in maroon cloth, lacking the errata slip, began appearing on the English market some time in the 1950s, their source Karl Germer who had inherited about 900 sets of sheets from Crowley's estate. Germer sold the majority to the occult publisher, Samuel Weiser, who affixed a cancel slip obliterating the 1936 imprint and reading 'Occult Research Press, 117 Fourth Avenue, New York 3, New York.'

50 MS note by Fra. N.·. in his wife's copy of BL7, Warburg.

51 loc. cit.

52 Presentation copy to John Bunting, inscribed by Crowley, 'the foundation of my life-work,' catalogued by the Redbridge Book Service, summer 1968.

53 Crowley to Fra. N.·., Paris, 3 May [1928], Warburg.

54 Gerald Yorke's 'Bibliography of the Works of Aleister Crowley' appended to John Symonds's *The Great Beast* (London, Rider, 1951), although not transcribing title pages or giving formats or print-runs, is of inestimable use. Edward Noel Fitzgerald's 'Works of Aleister Crowley Published or Privately Printed: a Bibliographical List' appended to Charles Richard Cammell, *Aleister Crowley: The Man, The Mage, the Poet* (London, Richards Press, 1951) is incomplete and marred by errors of transcription. G F Sims's rare book catalogue no. 12, *Magick: Books by the Master Therion* (Harrow, [1951]) offered ninety-nine Crowley items (acquired, though the catalogue does not say so, from the library of Sir Gerald Kelly) and is of vital if limited importance. Equally useful, but again restrictive, is Keith Hogg's sale-catalogue of the Crowley collection of Major-General J. F. C. Fuller (Tenterden, 1966) (acquired *en bloc* by the University of Texas, Austin). Will Parfitt and A. Drylie, *A Crowley Cross-Index* (Faulkland, Bath, Agape Magazine, 1976) is exactly what it says and has no bibliographical pretensions.

55 See Fredson Bowers, *Principles of Bibliographical Description* (New Jersey, Princeton University Press, 1949), p.151.

56 These two points are made by Dr Ian Fletcher in an anonymous essay in *The Times Literary Supplement,* 'A Study in Black and White: the Legend and Letters of Aubrey Beardsley,' 14 January 1972, p. 26.

57 J. C. T. Oates, 'Charles Edward Sayle', *Transactions of the Cambridge Bibliographical Society,* VIII (1982).

58 Cambridge University Library, MS. Res. b.1345(2).

59 The book, as we shall see, was printed in Paris. Copies were distributed by the London firm of Arthur Probsthain.

60 *Collected Works* (Foyers, 1905), I, 115-16.

61 G.F.Sims's catalogue no. 12 (Harrow [1951]), item 51. Its provenance, the library of Sir Gerald Kelly, suggests, however, it may not have reached its intended recipient. Beardsley died in 1898, the year *Aceldema* came out. Most likely, Crowley retained the copy after inscribing it and gave it later to Kelly's sister, Rose, whom he married in 1903.

62 I say 'consider' because no copy is known to have survived. Pollitt's and Gerald Kelly's have, the latter very rarely met with.

63 I.e. Victoria and Albert Museum, pencil drawing of a vignetted head, c.1910, ex. collection of Canon John Gray, whom Spare also drew.

64 Spare's A.·.A.·. enrolment form dated 10 July [1909] and annotated thus by Crowley in 1912; Pennsylvania State University Library .

65 These titles are suggested as being published by Smithers in Patrick Kearney, *The Private Case: an Annotated Bibliography of the Private Case Erotica in the British (Museum) Library* (London, J. Landesman, 1981), nos. 1563 and 1883.

66 E.g. *Raccolta universale della opere di Giorgio Baffo,* 'Cosmopoli', 1789.

67 The *double-entendre* of 'Ophelia Cox' is obvious, though unoriginal: the pseudonym had already been employed for a pornographic text of c.1890, *With Rod and Bum, or Sport in the West End of London.* 'Née Mrs Hunt' is a pun on the title of an erotic novel, *The Confessions of Nemesis Hunt* (3 volumes, 1902-6). Actually the uncorrected proofs, which are all that survive of *Alexandra,* misprint 'Cor' for 'Cox' and 'mc' for 'Mrs', but the joke is clear enough: page-proofs rubber-stamped by the printer and dated between 13 October

and 7 December 1906, Humanities Research Department, University of Texas, Austin. Information from Mr Peter Mendes, to whom I am indebted for this and other facts concerning Victorian clandestine printing.

68 The Pollitt-Michael Sadleir-R. A. Harari-W. G. Good copy, exhibited at the Victoria and Albert Beardsley exhibition, catalogue nos. 539-40; private collection, London.

69 Charles T. Jacobi, *Some Notes on Books and Printing: a Guide for Authors and Others* (London, Chiswick Press, 1892), p.16.

70 Private collection.

71 Information from Mr Peter Mendes.

72 Copies of this book are also found on machine-made paper.

73 Warburg Institute.

74 *Annual Register for...the Year 1899* (1900), ii, 73.

75 E.g., *The House of the Wolfings* (Reeves & Turner, 1889) and *The Roots of the Mountains* (1890).

76 For instance, *The Rape of the Lock* (1896) and its 'miniature' edition of 1897; Ernest Dowson, *Verses* (1896); Vincent O'Sullivan, *The Houses of Sin* (1897); Cyprian Cope, *Arabesques* (1899); Ethel M. de Foublanque, *A Chaplet of Love Poems* (1899).

77 op. cit., p. 890.

78 John Symonds, *The Great Beast: The Life of Aleister Crowley* (London, Rider, 1951), p.48.

79 That is for the first issue, 'Privately Printed, 1901.' When the sheets were reissued with a cancel title-leaf in 1907, they were bound in blue cloth.

80 That is for the first issue, London, Kegan Paul, 1902. When reissued in 1907, the sheets were bound in blue cloth uniform with the second issue of *The Mother's Tragedy.*

81 *Confessions*, op. cit.

82 Crowley to Gerald Kelly, [1903?], Fra. N.˙.'s transcript, Warburg. This was not the only publication in which he involved Kelly, whose sister, Rose, he had married in 1903, for Kelly appears to have designed the back-cover vignette of *Rosa Mundi*: 'I send you a R.M.' Crowley writes from Foyers on 29 August, 1905 (Fra. N.˙.'s transcript, Warburg). 'I don't think it's any odds having a non-Rodin vignette–I wanted you to have a hand in a thing entirely your sister's.' The three love-poems to Rose, *Rosa Mundi* (1905), *Rosa Coeli* and *Rosa Inferni* (1907), each had coloured lithograph frontispieces by Auguste Clot after Auguste Rodin. *Rodin in Rime,* also 1907, contained seven lithographs by Clot after Rodin.

83 London, 1923, the sixteen-page pamphlet, not the four-page leaflet with the same title printed in Tunis the same year.

84 Nevertheless he gave her one of the eleven copies of BL4; see p. 18, above.

85 Diary for 1 January 1924, Fra. N.˙.'s transcript, Warburg.

86 Paris, 19 February 1929, Warburg.

87 *Sic.* Fra. N.˙.'s transcript of manuscript notes in Crowley's personal copy, Warburg.

88 *The Last Ritual* (Brighton, 1947). Housman's order of service misprinted Ecclesiasticus for Ecclesiastes.

89 Apart from the handmade paper copies–Duncombe-Jewell suggests there were fifty– which bore the imprint 'privately issued'.

90 Letter from Crowley to Blackett, 11 November 1903, Kegan Paul archives, box 'Contracts C-D', University College London.

91 Kegan Paul's royalties ledger, C29, pp. 17-18, Kegan Paul archives, University College London. Duncombe-Jewell states the edition was of a thousand copies but the ledger records only two hundred.

92 loc. cit., pp.109, 128, 19, 126.

93 Introduction to Volume 7 of *The Ashley Library: a Catalogue of the Printed Books...Collected by Thomas James Wise*, 11 vols., 1922-1936.

94 'Edited, Revised and Enlarged by Jerry Kay,' Xeno Publishing Co., no place but probably San Francisco, 1967.

95 Only on early pressings. See Stephen Davis, *Hammer of the Gods: the Led Zeppelin Saga* (London, Sidgwick & Jackson, 1985), p. 99. The band's 'hippie' allegiance is proclaimed in the song, 'Going to California' on its untitled, fourth, album (1970).

96 See Vernon Joynson, *The Acid Trip: a Complete Guide to Psychedelic Music* (Todmorden, Babylon Books, 1984), pp. 87-8.

97 'Rave On, John Donne,' on *Inarticulate Speech of the Heart*. The record-sleeve accords thanks to L. Ron Hubbard, scientology as well as Crowleyanity apparently affording inspiration for popular musicians.

98 Stephen M. Gardner jr., 'The First Goodbye' in Jac L. Tharpe (ed.), *Elvis: Images and Fancies* (University Press of Mississippi, 1979), p. 72.

99 'Leo Vincey,' *The 'Rosicrucian' Scandal* [London, 1911]. Crowley has obligingly written out the solution to the anagram in Fra. N∴'s copy, now in the Warburg Institute: 'cunts rot'.

100 The dating of the three editions of *Amphora* is difficult. The Burns & Oates edition gives 1908 on the title-page and would seem, therefore, to pre-date the 'authoress and intimates' one which, although undated, we know from Major General J. F. C. Fuller's copy (University of Texas, Austin) to have appeared in 'New Year 1909'. However, the British Museum copyright copy of the Burns & Oates edition (11647.ff.55) was not received until 19 January 1909. In the reissue of the Burns & Oates sheets, retitled *Hail Mary*, Crowley gives 1909 as the original date of its publication. This reissue, by Wieland and Co., 3 Great James Street, W.C., is also undated but cannot be later than December 1912 when Wieland moved to Kensington (see footnote 29). The British Museum received its copy (press-mark 011650.de.68) on 29 December 1911, which suggests that it, like its predecessors, was issued to mark the New Year, 1912 in this case. The presentation copy to 'Gretchen' is in the Humanities Research Department, University of Texas, Austin.

101 *Confessions,* op. cit.

102 Renouard was very consistent about this. Apart from *Why Jesus Wept* (1904), which has no roman numerals, his preliminary paginations are regularly capitalized: *Snowdrops* paginates [4] I-XX, 1-168; *Clouds Without Water* [2] I-XXII, 1-144; *The Sword of Song* [8] I-XII, 1-196; *The World's Tragedy* [8] I-XLVIII, 1-148. Cf. Lecram's pagination of *Magick in Theory and Practice* [1930], I-XXXII, 1-438.

103 The fourth and last poem of the series, *Rosa Decidua,* issued to mark Crowley's and Rose Kelly's divorce and limited to twenty copies, is of different format–and content, come to that.

104 Paris, 1903, printed by Clarke & Bishop, 338 rue St Honoré, in an edition of two

hundred copies.

105 HM Customs to Mudd, 2 October 1924, Fra. N∴'s transcript, Warburg.

106 If other than visual evidence were needed to ascribe *Bagh* to Renouard's workshop, a proof copy in the collection of Mr Jimmy Page supplies it, for the pages are rubber-stamped with Renouard's name and address. 'Burnt' Crowley recorded in his diary for 25 March, 1924 (Fra. N∴'s transcript). Gerald Yorke in his 'Bibliography,' (op. cit., p. 304) ascribes the same fate to copies of *White Stains* and *Snowdrops from a Curate's Garden* but Crowley, who mentions these titles in the same diary entry and gives their print-runs, refers only to *Bagh* as suffering at Customs's hands. It seems, therefore, there were two separate destructions. Furthermore in a statement prepared for his lawyer during his unsuccessful libel action against Constable & Co. and Nina Hamnett, publisher and author of *Laughing Torso*, at which passages from *White Stains* were read out by defending counsel, Crowley declared: 'They were distributed from Zermatt Switzerland in August 1898 by a Professor of Psychiatry to whom I entrusted the edition.' Nevertheless *Snowdrops* is a desperately rare book which seems to suggest destruction at some time of a number of copies.

107 *Confessions*, p. 556.

108 *Confessions*, loc. cit.

109 Crowley to Quinn, 1 September 1913, MS. transcript by Fra. N∴ in his copy, Warburg. The four copies I have examined, the George Raffalovich–J. F. C. Fuller–Robert A. Gilbert copy, Fra. N∴'s, Victor Neuburg's (perhaps a proof) and my own (rebound) all have those pages intact.

110 *Confessions*, p. 745.

111 The items are listed in the sale catalogue of Quinn's library, Part 1 (A–C) (New York, The Anderson Galleries, 1923).

112 Fra. N∴'s set of proofs (Warburg), dated by Renouard 13 October 1906, as we can see from the misprints (some of which are dealt with in footnote 67 above), exhibits an early state of the text; Major-General Fuller's set (Humanities Research Department, University of Texas, Austin) stamped by Renouard 7 December 1906, a later one.

113 The book was typeset in England by the Ballantyne Press; the proofs, bound in red morocco, belonged to Fra. N∴ and are now in the Warburg Institute. In the volume Crowley has written: 'This volume belongs to me, Aleister Crowley. It was stolen from the table by my bed by the thief, Norman Mudd, and has since passed through several larcenous hands...' This copy is believed to be unique.

114 Later reduced to six volumes; the prospectus of the abortive six-volume edition to be issued by Herbert Clarke, 338 rue St-Honoré, Paris (who had printed Crowley's *Berashith* in 1903) announces a supplementary seventh volume to be distributed *gratis* to subscribers.

115 See my *R. A. Caton and the Fortune Press* (London, Bertram Rota, 1983), p. 67.

116 Ten copies on Maillol handmade paper with the shields in gold and colour; forty with the shields in colour only; and 450 uncoloured copies.

117 As Smithers had, with illustrations by Aubrey Beardsley. Pollitt owned some of the original drawings.

118 Lindsay in Edward Nehls, *D.H. Lawrence: a Composite Biography* (University of Wisconsin Press, 1959), III, 301.

119 Quoted in Nehls, op. cit., III, 327.

120 Fra. N∴, Karl Germer, and perhaps Pearl Brookesmith.

121 Jack Lindsay, *Fanfrolico and After* (London, Bodley Head, 1962), p.172.

122 There is no printed limitation notice but Crowley has inscribed Fra. N∴'s copy 'No. 8 of 11 copies. Fratri V.I. from T.M.Θ. An Ixii [Sun] in O° [Libra] (i.e. the autumn equinox, 1938).' T.M.Θ. stands for 'To Mega Therion,' or Great Wild Beast.

123 Letter to Calder-Marshall, 2 February 1930, Fra. N∴'s transcript, Warburg.

124 Botolph was the firm that had produced *The Paintings of D.H. Lawrence* for the Mandrake Press.

125 Letter from Crowley to Fra. N∴, 10 August [1941], Warburg.

126 Regardie, op. cit., IV, 137-257.

127 Enough remained for it to be used to bind the twenty 'specials' of Crowley's swan-song, *Olla: an Anthology of Sixty Years of Song* (1946).

128 E.g. his vellum copy of *Carmen Saeculare* (1901) now in the Warburg Institute.

129 Crowley to Fra. N∴, Aston Clinton, 2 November 1944, Warburg.

130 The title recalls that of a popular and much-reprinted Victorian nursery primer, *Reading without Tears*.

131 Not the bird but the Italian word for 'whence', i.e. a secret location.

132 The poems' titles are 'A Conjuration of the Elements', 'Hymn to Tahuti', 'The Insensitive', 'A Meditation upon Gayatri', 'The Hermit', 'Cradle Song', and 'Elegy Written in a Country Farmyard'.

Notes To Chapter Four.

1 Quoted from a leaflet entitled *My Aim* which Chubb issued in 1929.

2 An exception might, however, be made with the work of the German artist Otto Schoff (1884-1938). His series of lithographs, 'Knabenliebe', displays a salaciousness not present in Chubb's work, but his selection of the poems of Platen, *Der verfehmte Eros*, published in Berlin by Fritz Gurlitt in 1921 as No. 7 of a series called 'Das geschriebene Buch', is a lithographic reproduction of Schoff's text and illustrations curiously akin, in technique and subject-matter, to Chubb's productions.

3 Quoted from the unique manuscript, *The Book of Nature and Supernature* (1930), but repeated with slight variations in several other places.

4 R. N. Chubb, *Note on Some Water-Colour Drawings (exhibited at the Goupil Gallery)* (London, 1929), a four-page leaflet. There are two issues, one of which omits the penultimate paragraph quoted here.

5 Peter F. Anson, *Bishops at Large* (London, 1964), p.493.

6 *Sunday Chronicle*, 3 October 1954.

7 He was consecrated Bishop by Hugh George de Willmott Newman, otherwise known as His Sacred Beatitude Mar Georgius I, Patriarch of Glastonbury, Caertroia and Mylapore, Successor of St Thomas, Apostolic Pontiff of Celtica and the Indies, Prince Catholicos of the West, and of the United Orthodox Catholic Rite, in the somewhat unecclesiastical setting of the Juvenile Courtroom, Vauxhall Bridge Road. For an account of his mystical and religious activities see Anson, *Bishops at Large,* pp.492-5 and Henry R. T. Brandreth, *Episcopi Vagantes and the Anglican Church,* 2nd ed. (London, 1961), p. 83.

Index